The Art of Extre

How to Live on Almos ___ng and Thrive

by Sergio Rijo

While every precaution has been taken in the preparation of this book, the publisher assumes no responsibility for errors or omissions, or for damages resulting from the use of the information contained herein.

THE ART OF EXTREME BUDGETING: HOW TO LIVE ON ALMOST NOTHING AND THRIVE

First edition. May 2, 2023.

ISBN: 979-8223507000

Written by SERGIO RIJO.

Table of Contents

Chapter 1: Introduction

As someone who has experienced the ups and downs of managing finances, I know firsthand the importance of budgeting. In fact, I've come to learn that extreme budgeting can be a lifesaver. But what is extreme budgeting, and why is it so important?

For me, extreme budgeting is about finding ways to live on almost nothing while still enjoying life to the fullest. It means taking a hard look at your expenses, making tough choices, and being disciplined about your spending habits. It may not be easy, but it's certainly possible.

Why is extreme budgeting important? Well, for starters, it can help you get out of debt and stay out of debt. It can also help you save money for emergencies, invest in your future, and even achieve financial freedom. Plus, by living on less, you're able to reduce your environmental footprint and live a more minimalist lifestyle.

But I'll be honest: extreme budgeting isn't for everyone. It takes a lot of effort, discipline, and sacrifice. It may mean saying no to certain luxuries and living a simpler life. But if you're willing to put in the work, the rewards can be tremendous.

That's why I wrote this book. My goal is to provide practical tips and strategies for extreme budgeting, based on my own experiences and those of others who have successfully lived on almost nothing. I want to show you that it's possible to thrive, even when your budget is tight.

Throughout this book, we'll cover a range of topics, from assessing your financial situation and getting rid of debt, to finding extra income, reducing expenses, and even living a minimalist lifestyle. We'll also talk about how to eat, shop, travel, and entertain yourself on a budget. And we'll explore the power of planning, time management, and building a support network to help you stay on track.

My hope is that this book will inspire you to take control of your finances, live a more intentional life, and embrace the art of extreme budgeting. Let's get started.

Chapter 2: Assessing Your Financial Situation

As we dive into the world of extreme budgeting, it's important to take a step back and assess our current financial situation. This can be a daunting task, but it's essential to lay a foundation for our journey towards financial freedom.

To begin, we need to get a clear understanding of our current financial standing. This means taking a detailed look at our income, expenses, debts, and assets. It's easy to ignore our finances and put off this task, but the longer we wait, the harder it becomes to dig ourselves out of any financial holes we may have dug.

Once we have a clear picture of our finances, the next step is to create a budget. This may seem like a restrictive task, but in reality, it's liberating. When we have a budget, we have control over our money, and we can allocate funds towards our goals and priorities. Our budget is a roadmap that guides us towards financial success.

When creating a budget, it's essential to be honest and realistic. We need to account for all of our expenses, from the necessities like housing and food, to the luxuries like entertainment and travel. We also need to be honest with ourselves about our spending habits. Are there areas where we tend to overspend? Are there any expenses that we can cut back on?

Identifying areas where we can cut back is the next step towards financial freedom. This can be a challenging task, as we may be attached to certain luxuries and habits that we believe are essential to our well-being. However, it's important to remember that extreme budgeting isn't about deprivation or living a life of constant sacrifice. It's about being intentional with our money and making choices that align with our priorities.

There are many areas where we can cut back on expenses. For example, we can take a closer look at our grocery bill and find ways to save money on food. This may mean meal planning, cooking at home more often, or shopping at a more affordable grocery store. We can also look for ways to reduce our transportation costs, such as carpooling or using public transportation.

We may also need to make some tough choices about our spending habits. Are we spending money on subscriptions or memberships that we don't use? Do we need to cut back on eating out or buying new clothes? These choices may be difficult, but they can have a significant impact on our financial situation.

Assessing our financial situation, creating a budget, and identifying areas where we can cut back are critical steps towards extreme budgeting. These steps may require some time and effort, but they are essential for achieving financial freedom. By being intentional with our money and making choices that align with our priorities, we can live a fulfilling and abundant life while still sticking to a budget.

Chapter 3: Getting Rid of Debt

Debt can be a heavy burden, weighing down on you and preventing you from achieving your financial goals. But getting rid of debt can be a liberating experience, allowing you to regain control of your finances and work towards a brighter future. In this chapter, we'll explore how to create a debt payoff plan, identify strategies to pay off debt quickly, and stay motivated throughout the process.

Creating a debt payoff plan starts with understanding your current debt situation. This means gathering all your debt statements, including credit cards, loans, and other forms of debt. Write down the name of the creditor, the outstanding balance, the interest rate, and the minimum payment required. Once you have a clear picture of your debt, you can start creating a plan to pay it off.

The next step is to identify strategies to pay off debt quickly. One effective method is the debt snowball method, where you focus on paying off the smallest debt first and then moving on to the next smallest debt until all your debts are paid off. Another method is the debt avalanche method, where you focus on paying off the debt with the highest interest rate first and then moving on to the next highest interest rate debt until all your debts are paid off.

Whichever method you choose, it's important to stay motivated throughout the debt payoff process. This can be challenging, as debt repayment can take time and require discipline and sacrifice. One way to stay motivated is to celebrate small victories along the way. For example, when you pay off a debt, take a moment to acknowledge the progress you've made and reward yourself with something small, like a cup of coffee or a movie rental.

Another way to stay motivated is to track your progress visually. Create a chart or graph that shows your debt decreasing over time, and update it regularly as you make payments. Seeing the progress you've made can be incredibly motivating, and can help you stay on track towards your debt payoff goal.

It's also important to remind yourself of why you're working so hard to pay off your debt. Maybe you want to buy a house, start a business, or travel the world. Whatever your goal is, keep it in mind and let it motivate you to keep going, even when the going gets tough.

In addition to these strategies, there are some practical steps you can take to make debt repayment easier. For example, consider consolidating your debt into a single loan with a lower interest rate. This can make it easier to manage your debt and reduce the amount of interest you pay over time.

Another option is to negotiate with your creditors to see if you can get a lower interest rate or a payment plan that works better for your budget. Many creditors are willing to work with you if you're upfront and honest about your financial situation.

Finally, consider seeking support from others who are going through the same process. Join a debt support group or online community where you can share your struggles and successes with others who understand what you're going through. Having a support network can make all the difference when it comes to staying motivated and making progress towards your debt payoff goal.

Getting rid of debt is a challenging but rewarding process. By creating a debt payoff plan, identifying strategies to pay off debt quickly, and staying motivated throughout the process, you can take control of your finances and work towards a brighter financial future.

Chapter 4: Finding Extra Income

Are you struggling to make ends meet even after creating a budget and cutting back on expenses? You are not alone. Many of us find ourselves in a situation where we need to make extra income to pay off debt or simply to make ends meet. In this chapter, we will explore some ways to find extra income and put your skills and talents to use.

Identifying sources of extra income

There are many sources of extra income that you can tap into. Here are a few ideas to get you started:

Online freelancing: If you have a skill that can be done remotely, consider freelancing online. Websites like Upwork, Fiverr, and Freelancer.com offer a platform for you to showcase your skills and find clients. Whether you're a writer, graphic designer, or programmer, there's a chance you can find work online.

Part-time work: Look for part-time work that suits your schedule. You could work in a retail store, restaurant, or even a delivery service. Keep in mind that part-time work doesn't always pay well, but it can be a great way to supplement your income.

Rent out your space: If you have a spare room or parking space, you can rent it out on platforms like Airbnb or ParkingSpotter. This can be a great source of extra income, especially if you live in a popular tourist destination.

Sell items you don't need: If you have items that you don't use or need, consider selling them. You could sell them on eBay, Craigslist, or Facebook Marketplace. Not only will you make extra money, but you'll also declutter your space.

Creative ways to make money

If you're willing to put in a little more effort, here are some creative ways to make money:

Dog walking: If you love dogs and enjoy spending time outdoors, consider offering dog-walking services. You could advertise your services in local community groups or on social media.

Babysitting: If you enjoy spending time with kids, consider offering babysitting services. You could also advertise your services in local community groups or on social media.

Food delivery: If you have a reliable vehicle, you could sign up to deliver food for services like Uber Eats or DoorDash. This can be a great way to earn extra money in your spare time.

Virtual tutoring: If you have expertise in a particular subject, you could offer virtual tutoring services. This can be a great way to share your knowledge and earn extra income.

How to use your talents and skills to earn extra income

Another way to make extra income is to use your talents and skills. Here are some ideas to get you started:

Photography: If you're a skilled photographer, consider offering your services for events like weddings or corporate functions. You could also sell your photos online on websites like Shutterstock or iStock.

Writing: If you're a skilled writer, consider offering your services for blog writing or copywriting. You could also write and self-publish a book or an e-book.

Music: If you're a talented musician, consider offering your services for events like weddings or corporate functions. You could also teach music lessons or record your own music.

Crafts: If you're skilled at crafting, consider selling your creations online or at local markets. You could also offer your services for custom orders.

There are many ways to make extra income, and you don't have to be limited to traditional part-time work. Get creative and put your skills and talents to use. Remember, the key is to find something that you enjoy and that suits your schedule. With some hard work and dedication, you can find extra income and improve your financial situation.

Chapter 5: Reducing Expenses

In today's world, it is easy to fall into the trap of overspending. With advertisements and peer pressure to have the latest gadgets, fashionable clothes, and luxurious vacations, it can be challenging to keep your spending in check. However, excessive spending can lead to a life of stress, anxiety, and debt. This is why identifying unnecessary expenses, cutting back on bills, and saving money on everyday expenses are essential to extreme budgeting. In this chapter, I will share some practical tips to help you reduce your expenses and live a fulfilling life within your means.

Identifying Unnecessary Expenses

The first step to reducing expenses is identifying what expenses are unnecessary. Many of us may not even realize how much money we are spending on things we do not need. It is crucial to evaluate your spending habits and identify where you can cut back. Here are some common expenses that you can easily reduce:

Eating out: Eating out regularly can be expensive. Preparing meals at home can save you a lot of money in the long run. Instead of dining out, try cooking at home, and bring your lunch to work.

Cable TV: With the advent of streaming services, cable TV has become less of a necessity. Consider canceling your cable TV subscription and switching to a streaming service.

Gym membership: Many people pay for gym memberships but never use them. If you are not using your gym membership regularly, consider canceling it and finding other ways to stay active.

Impulse purchases: Impulse purchases are often the result of emotional triggers such as boredom, stress, or peer pressure. Try to avoid impulse purchases and only buy things that you need.

Cutting Back on Bills

Cutting back on bills can be a daunting task, but it is one of the most effective ways to reduce your expenses. Here are some tips to help you cut back on your bills:

Energy bills: Reduce your energy bills by turning off lights and appliances when you are not using them. You can also invest in energy-efficient appliances and light bulbs.

Phone bills: Shop around for the best phone plans that fit your needs. Consider switching to a pay-as-you-go plan or a plan with a lower data cap if you are not using your phone regularly.

Insurance bills: Shop around for the best insurance rates. Consider bundling your insurance policies with one company to save money.

Credit card bills: Pay off your credit card balance in full each month to avoid interest charges. If you are carrying a balance, consider transferring it to a card with a lower interest rate.

Saving Money on Everyday Expenses

Saving money on everyday expenses can add up over time. Here are some tips to help you save money on your everyday expenses:

Grocery shopping: Make a list before you go grocery shopping and stick to it. Buy generic or store-brand products instead of name-brand products. You can also consider buying in bulk to save money.

Transportation: Use public transportation or carpool with friends to save money on gas and parking.

Clothing: Shop during off-season sales to get discounts on clothing. You can also consider buying second-hand clothes at thrift stores.

Entertainment: Look for free or low-cost entertainment options in your community. You can also borrow books and movies from the library instead of buying them.

Reducing expenses is an essential part of extreme budgeting. By identifying unnecessary expenses, cutting back on bills, and saving money on everyday expenses, you can significantly reduce your expenses and live within your means. Remember, it is not about depriving yourself of the things you love, but rather finding ways to enjoy life without breaking the bank.

Chapter 6: Living a Minimalist Lifestyle

Living a minimalist lifestyle has become a popular trend in recent years, and for good reason. It can be an incredibly effective way to reduce stress, increase happiness, and save money. In this chapter, we'll explore the benefits of living a minimalist lifestyle, offer tips for decluttering, and provide strategies for how to live with less.

The Benefits of Living a Minimalist Lifestyle

At its core, minimalism is about simplicity. It's about focusing on what truly matters and getting rid of anything that doesn't contribute to your happiness or well-being. By living a minimalist lifestyle, you can experience a number of benefits, including:

Reduced stress: When you have fewer possessions, you have fewer things to worry about. You don't have to spend as much time cleaning, organizing, or maintaining your stuff, which can free up more time and energy for the things that really matter.

More money: When you're not constantly buying new things, you can save a lot of money. This can give you more financial freedom and allow you to pursue your passions without worrying about money as much.

Increased happiness: Many people find that living a minimalist lifestyle leads to increased happiness. When you're not constantly chasing after material possessions, you can focus on cultivating meaningful relationships, pursuing your hobbies, and finding joy in the simple things in life.

Tips for Decluttering

If you're interested in living a minimalist lifestyle, the first step is to declutter your home. Here are some tips to help you get started:

Start small: Don't try to declutter your entire home all at once. Instead, start with one room or one category of items, such as your clothes or your books.

Set goals: Decide what you want to accomplish with your decluttering efforts. Do you want to get rid of a certain percentage of your belongings? Do you want to create a more organized and functional space? Having clear goals can help keep you motivated.

Be ruthless: When you're decluttering, be honest with yourself about what you really need and what you can do without. If you haven't used something in a year or more, it's probably safe to get rid of it.

Consider the environmental impact: When you're getting rid of things, think about where they will end up. Can you donate them to a charity or sell them online? Can you recycle them? Try to avoid sending things to the landfill whenever possible.

How to Live with Less

Once you've decluttered your home, the next step is to learn how to live with less. Here are some strategies to help you get started:

Buy only what you need: Before you make a purchase, ask yourself if you really need the item in question. If the answer is no, don't buy it.

Focus on experiences, not possessions: Instead of spending money on things, focus on experiences. Take a trip, try a new hobby, or spend time with friends and family.

Find joy in the simple things: Living a minimalist lifestyle doesn't mean you have to give up all forms of luxury or enjoyment. Instead, focus on finding joy in the simple things in life, like a good book or a beautiful sunset.

Embrace imperfection: Living a minimalist lifestyle doesn't mean you have to be perfect. It's okay to have clutter from time to time or to make the occasional frivolous purchase. What matters most is that you're mindful of your possessions and your spending habits.

Living a minimalist lifestyle can be a powerful way to reduce stress, save money, and increase happiness. By decluttering your home and learning to live with less, you can focus on what truly matters and find joy in the simple things in life. It may not be easy at first, but with practice and dedication, anyone can adopt a minimalist mindset and enjoy the benefits that come with it.

Remember, minimalism is not about deprivation or austerity. It's about creating space for the things that truly matter in your life, whether that's spending time with loved ones, pursuing a passion, or simply enjoying a quiet moment of reflection. By embracing simplicity and letting go of excess, you can create a more meaningful and fulfilling life.

So, take a deep breath, look around your home, and start thinking about what you really need to be happy. You may be surprised by how little it actually takes to live a rich and rewarding life. And who knows, you may even find that you enjoy the process of decluttering and simplifying your life more than you ever thought possible.

Chapter 7: Eating on a Budget

Eating healthy, nutritious meals is important for our physical and mental well-being. However, many people believe that eating healthy is expensive and therefore, unattainable. In this chapter, we'll explore the importance of eating on a budget, provide tips for meal planning, shopping for groceries on a budget, and cooking healthy, affordable meals.

Why Eating on a Budget is Important

Eating on a budget is crucial for several reasons. Firstly, it can save you a significant amount of money. According to the Bureau of Labor Statistics, food is one of the largest household expenses, with the average American family spending over $7,700 per year on food alone. By learning how to eat on a budget, you can significantly reduce your grocery bill and allocate your money towards other important expenses, such as rent, healthcare, and education.

Secondly, eating on a budget can help you maintain a healthy weight and reduce the risk of chronic diseases. By cooking your meals at home and incorporating more fruits, vegetables, and whole grains into your diet, you can control the ingredients and portions of your meals, leading to better health outcomes.

Meal Planning

Meal planning is a crucial component of eating on a budget. It involves deciding what meals you'll be eating for the week and making a shopping list based on those meals. Here are some tips for effective meal planning:

Plan your meals around the weekly grocery ads: Take a look at the weekly grocery ads to see what's on sale. Plan your meals around those items to save money.

Cook in bulk: Cook large batches of food and freeze leftovers. This will save you time and money in the long run.

Use seasonal produce: Seasonal produce is often cheaper and fresher than out-of-season produce. Plan your meals around seasonal produce to save money and eat healthier.

Incorporate pantry staples: Use pantry staples, such as beans, rice, and pasta, in your meals to save money.

Shopping for Groceries on a Budget

Once you've planned your meals, it's time to go grocery shopping. Here are some tips for shopping for groceries on a budget:

Stick to your list: Make a shopping list based on your meal plan and stick to it. Avoid impulse purchases, which can add up quickly.

Shop the perimeter: The perimeter of the grocery store usually contains fresh produce, meat, and dairy products. These items are usually healthier and cheaper than processed foods.

Buy in bulk: Buy items in bulk, such as rice, pasta, and canned goods. This can be much cheaper than buying individual items.

Use coupons: Look for coupons in the weekly ads or online. Use them to save money on items you need.

Cooking Healthy, Affordable Meals

Cooking healthy, affordable meals is easier than you might think. Here are some tips to get started:

Keep it simple: Stick to simple recipes with few ingredients. This will save you time and money.

Use plant-based proteins: Plant-based proteins, such as beans and lentils, are cheaper and healthier than meat.

Use herbs and spices: Use herbs and spices to add flavor to your meals instead of expensive sauces and seasonings.

Make your own snacks: Make your own snacks, such as granola bars and trail mix. This is cheaper and healthier than buying pre-packaged snacks.

Eating on a budget is important for your financial and physical well-being. By meal planning, shopping for groceries on a budget, and cooking healthy, affordable meals, you can save money and maintain a healthy lifestyle. Remember, eating healthy doesn't have to be expensive. With a little planning and creativity, you can enjoy delicious, nutritious meals without breaking the bank.

It's also important to keep in mind that eating on a budget is a continuous process. It takes practice and patience to learn how to make the most of your grocery budget. But the rewards are well worth it. Not only will you save money, but you'll also feel better and have more energy to take on life's challenges.

Chapter 8: Housing on a Budget

Finding a place to call home is one of the most fundamental human needs. However, with the rising cost of living, housing has become increasingly expensive, making it difficult for many people to find affordable options. In this chapter, we'll explore the different options for housing on a budget, including renting vs. owning, alternative housing options, and finding affordable housing.

Renting vs. Owning

One of the biggest decisions when it comes to housing is whether to rent or own. Both options have their advantages and disadvantages, and the decision ultimately depends on your personal financial situation and lifestyle.

Renting can be a good option for those who are not ready to commit to a long-term investment, do not have the means for a down payment, or prefer the flexibility of being able to move easily. Renting also typically includes maintenance and repair costs that are covered by the landlord, which can be a significant savings.

Owning a home, on the other hand, can provide long-term stability and the potential for building equity. Homeownership also allows for greater control over the property, the ability to make renovations, and the potential for rental income. However, homeownership comes with added expenses, such as property taxes, maintenance and repairs, and potentially a mortgage payment.

Alternative Housing Options

If neither renting nor owning is a viable option for you, there are alternative housing options to consider. Here are a few:

Tiny Houses: Tiny houses have become increasingly popular as a way to downsize and live a more minimalistic lifestyle. These small homes typically range from 100 to 400 square feet and can be built on a trailer or on a foundation.

Co-living: Co-living is a shared housing arrangement in which individuals or families share a living space, often with shared amenities and communal areas. This can be a good option for those who want to save money on rent while also building community.

Mobile Homes: Mobile homes, also known as manufactured homes, can be a more affordable option for those who want the benefits of homeownership without the high cost. These homes can be moved and are typically less expensive than traditional homes.

Finding Affordable Housing

No matter what housing option you choose, finding affordable housing can be a challenge. Here are some tips for finding affordable housing:

Research online: Use online resources to search for affordable housing options in your area. Websites like Zillow, Trulia, and Craigslist can be a good place to start.

Talk to local housing authorities: Local housing authorities can provide information on affordable housing options, including government-funded programs, low-income housing, and subsidies.

Consider roommates: Sharing living space with roommates can significantly lower the cost of rent and utilities.

Look outside of urban areas: Housing in urban areas is often more expensive than in suburban or rural areas. Consider looking outside of the city to find more affordable options.

Housing is a fundamental aspect of our lives, but it can also be a significant financial burden. By exploring alternative housing options and being strategic about renting or owning, you can find affordable housing that meets your needs. Remember, housing doesn't have to break the bank, and with some creativity and research, you can find a comfortable and affordable place to call home.

Chapter 9: Transportation on a Budget

Transportation is an essential part of our daily lives, allowing us to commute to work, travel, and run errands. However, it can also be one of the most significant expenses we face. From car payments to gas, insurance, and maintenance, the cost of transportation can quickly add up. In this chapter, we'll explore ways to cut transportation costs, choose affordable transportation options, and maintain your vehicle on a budget.

Cutting Transportation Costs

Cutting transportation costs is an effective way to save money and improve your financial situation. Here are some tips to help you reduce your transportation expenses:

Carpooling

Carpooling is an excellent way to save money on gas and maintenance costs. By sharing a ride with friends or coworkers, you can reduce your transportation expenses significantly. Not only does carpooling save you money, but it also helps reduce traffic congestion and air pollution.

Public Transportation

Public transportation is a cost-effective way to travel, especially in urban areas. Taking the bus or train instead of driving can save you money on gas, maintenance, and parking fees. Additionally, many public transportation systems offer discounts for seniors, students, and low-income individuals.

Walking and Biking

Walking or biking is not only a cost-effective transportation option, but it's also great for your health. If you live close to your workplace or frequently visited locations, consider walking or biking instead of driving. It's an excellent way to save money on gas and maintenance costs while staying fit.

Choosing Affordable Transportation Options

Choosing affordable transportation options is essential for those who cannot afford to purchase a car or are looking to save money. Here are some affordable transportation options to consider:

Used Cars

If you're in the market for a car, consider purchasing a used vehicle instead of a new one. Used cars are often much cheaper than new cars and can provide excellent value for your money. Be sure to research the car's history, take it for a test drive, and have a mechanic inspect it before making a purchase.

Scooters and Motorcycles

Scooters and motorcycles are an affordable transportation option for those who don't need a car. They're excellent for short commutes and can save you money on gas and maintenance costs. However, be sure to check your state's regulations and requirements before purchasing a scooter or motorcycle.

Electric Bikes

Electric bikes are an eco-friendly and affordable transportation option. They're perfect for short commutes and can save you money on gas and maintenance costs. Additionally, many electric bike models are foldable, making them easy to store and transport.

Maintaining Your Vehicle on a Budget

Maintaining your vehicle on a budget is essential to prevent costly repairs down the road. Here are some tips to help you maintain your vehicle on a budget:

Regular Maintenance

Regular maintenance is essential to keep your car running smoothly and prevent costly repairs. Be sure to follow your car's manufacturer recommendations for oil changes, tire rotations, and other routine maintenance tasks.

DIY Repairs

Some minor repairs can be done at home, saving you money on labor costs. Learn how to change your car's oil, replace brake pads, and change air filters. However, be sure to research the repair before attempting it and have a mechanic inspect your work to ensure it's done correctly.

Shop Around

When it's time to take your car in for repairs, shop around for the best price. Compare prices and reviews from multiple mechanics in your area before making a decision.

Transportation is an essential part of our lives, but it doesn't have to break the bank. By carpooling, taking public transportation, walking or biking, and choosing affordable transportation options, you can significantly reduce your transportation expenses. Additionally, maintaining your vehicle on a budget can prevent costly repairs down the road.

It's important to remember that transportation expenses are not fixed and can vary greatly depending on your choices and habits. By being mindful of your transportation choices and implementing some of the tips mentioned in this chapter, you can save money and improve your financial situation.

It's also worth noting that transportation choices can have an impact on the environment. Choosing eco-friendly transportation options like electric bikes, walking, and public transportation can help reduce air pollution and carbon emissions.

In summary, when it comes to transportation on a budget, there are many options available. From carpooling and public transportation to walking and biking, there are ways to cut transportation costs and save money. Additionally, choosing affordable transportation options like used cars, scooters, and electric bikes can provide excellent value for your money. And, maintaining your vehicle on a budget can prevent costly repairs and help extend its lifespan.

Remember, small changes in your transportation habits and choices can add up to significant savings in the long run. By being mindful of your expenses and implementing some of the tips in this chapter, you can improve your financial situation and make a positive impact on the environment.

Chapter 10: Entertainment on a Budget

Entertainment is an essential aspect of our lives. It is the escape we need from our busy schedules and a way to relax and unwind. However, entertainment can be costly, and many people find themselves sacrificing their hobbies and interests to save money. But with a little creativity and effort, it is possible to enjoy entertainment without breaking the bank. In this chapter, we'll explore ways to find free and low-cost entertainment, creative ways to have fun without spending money, and how to make memories without breaking the bank.

Finding Free and Low-Cost Entertainment

Entertainment does not have to cost a fortune. Many free or low-cost options are available, and you can still have fun without spending a lot of money. Here are some ways to find free and low-cost entertainment:

Local Events

Check your local newspaper, community bulletin boards, or social media groups for free events in your area. Many communities host free events such as concerts, festivals, and outdoor movie screenings. Attending these events can be an excellent way to have fun and meet new people without spending any money.

Museums and Galleries

Many museums and galleries offer free admission on specific days or times. Take advantage of these opportunities to explore art and history without spending a dime. Additionally, many museums and galleries offer discounted admission to students, seniors, and military personnel.

Parks and Trails

Parks and trails are a great way to enjoy the outdoors and get some exercise. Many parks and trails offer free admission, and some even have free equipment rental for activities like kayaking, hiking, and biking.

Creative Ways to Have Fun Without Spending Money

There are many creative ways to have fun without spending money. Here are some ideas to get you started:

Game Night

Hosting a game night is a great way to have fun with friends and family without spending money. Ask everyone to bring their favorite board game, and you'll have hours of fun without spending a dime.

Movie Night

Instead of going to the theater, have a movie night at home. Rent a movie from the library or streaming service, make some popcorn, and snuggle up on the couch for a cozy night in.

Cooking Competition

Have a cooking competition with your friends or family. Each person can bring their favorite dish, and you can judge who made the best meal. It's a fun way to spend time together and try new foods without spending a lot of money.

Making Memories Without Breaking the Bank

You don't need to spend a lot of money to make memories. Here are some ideas to help you create lasting memories without breaking the bank:

Picnics

Pack a picnic lunch and head to a nearby park or beach for a fun and inexpensive outing. Bring a frisbee, football, or other games to play while you enjoy your meal.

Road Trips

Take a road trip to a nearby destination for a day or weekend getaway. Pack a lunch and snacks, and explore the area's natural beauty and attractions.

Volunteer Work

Volunteer work can be a fulfilling and rewarding way to make memories while helping others. Many organizations offer volunteer opportunities for a variety of interests, from working with animals to assisting at a food bank.

Entertainment is an essential part of our lives, and it doesn't have to be expensive. By finding free and low-cost entertainment, getting creative with your hobbies and interests, and making memories without breaking the bank, you can enjoy your downtime without sacrificing your financial goals. Remember, the best things in life are often free, and the memories you make with loved ones will last a lifetime.

Chapter 11: Saving for Emergencies

Emergencies can happen to anyone, at any time. Whether it's a sudden job loss, a medical emergency, or a car accident, unexpected expenses can throw even the most carefully planned budget off track. That's why having an emergency fund is essential. In this chapter, we'll explore why emergency savings are important, how to build an emergency fund, and strategies for staying motivated to save.

Why Emergency Savings are Important

Emergency savings are a crucial component of financial stability. Having a cushion of money set aside for unexpected expenses can help you avoid going into debt or relying on credit cards to cover unforeseen costs. Emergency savings can also help alleviate the stress and anxiety that can come with a sudden financial crisis.

Without emergency savings, you may be forced to tap into retirement accounts, take out loans, or use credit cards to cover expenses. These options can lead to long-term financial consequences, such as high-interest debt, penalties, and decreased retirement savings.

How to Build an Emergency Fund

Building an emergency fund takes time and discipline, but it's a worthwhile investment in your financial future. Here are some tips to help you build an emergency fund:

Set a Savings Goal

The first step to building an emergency fund is to set a savings goal. Aim to save three to six months' worth of living expenses in case of a job loss or other financial emergency. If that seems daunting, start with a smaller goal, such as saving $1,000.

Create a Budget

Creating a budget is essential to identify areas where you can cut back on spending and redirect those funds towards your emergency savings. Look for opportunities to save money on groceries, entertainment, and other non-essential expenses.

Automate Savings

One of the easiest ways to save money is to automate your savings. Set up a direct deposit from your paycheck to a separate savings account designated for emergencies. This way, a portion of your paycheck will go directly into your emergency fund without you having to think about it.

Sell Unwanted Items

Selling unwanted items can be a great way to jumpstart your emergency fund. Hold a garage sale, sell items online, or donate items to a thrift store for a tax deduction.

Strategies for Staying Motivated

Building an emergency fund can be challenging, but there are strategies you can use to stay motivated and on track. Here are some tips to help you stay committed to your savings goal:

Visualize Your Goal

Visualizing your savings goal can be a powerful motivator. Imagine what it will feel like to have a cushion of money set aside for emergencies. Focus on the peace of mind that comes with knowing you're financially prepared for unexpected expenses.

Track Your Progress

Tracking your progress can help you stay motivated and celebrate small victories along the way. Use a spreadsheet or budgeting app to monitor your savings and watch your emergency fund grow.

Celebrate Milestones

Celebrating milestones is a great way to stay motivated and keep your savings goal top of mind. When you reach a savings milestone, treat yourself to a small reward, like a night out or a new book.

Stay Committed

Building an emergency fund takes time and discipline, but it's worth the effort. Stay committed to your savings goal, even when it feels challenging. Remember why you're saving and the peace of mind that comes with having a cushion of money set aside for emergencies.

Building an emergency fund is an essential step towards financial stability. With a little planning, discipline, and motivation, you can create a cushion of money to help you weather unexpected expenses. Remember to set a savings goal, create a budget, automate savings, sell unwanted items, visualize your goal, track your progress, celebrate milestones, and stay committed. With these strategies, you can build an emergency fund that will provide peace of mind and financial security. By taking the time to invest in your emergency fund, you can protect yourself and your family from the stress and financial strain that comes with unexpected expenses.

Remember that emergencies can happen to anyone, regardless of income or financial situation. Even if you're living paycheck to paycheck, it's still possible to build an emergency fund. Start with small savings goals and work your way up. Every little bit helps, and over time, your emergency fund will grow.

In addition to building an emergency fund, it's important to have a plan in place for how you'll use the funds in case of an emergency. Consider what types of expenses you may need to cover and how much you'll need to have set aside. It can also be helpful to consult with a financial advisor or trusted friend or family member to help you create a plan.

Finally, remember that building an emergency fund is just one aspect of financial planning. It's important to continue to prioritize savings, budgeting, and investing for the long term. By taking a proactive approach to your finances, you can create a solid foundation for a bright financial future.

Building an emergency fund is an essential component of financial stability. By setting a savings goal, creating a budget, automating savings, selling unwanted items, visualizing your goal, tracking your progress, celebrating milestones, and staying committed, you can create a cushion of money to help you weather unexpected expenses. Remember that emergencies can happen to anyone, and it's never too late to start building your emergency fund. With a little planning, discipline, and motivation, you can protect yourself and your family from the stress and financial strain that comes with unexpected expenses.

Chapter 12: Investing on a Budget

Investing is often associated with wealth, but it's a misconception that only the rich can invest. Investing can be a powerful tool to build wealth, even for those on a tight budget. In this chapter, we'll explore the benefits of investing, how to start investing with little money, and low-cost investment options.

The Benefits of Investing

Investing is the process of putting money into something with the expectation of receiving a return on that investment. While investing can involve risks, it also has the potential for significant rewards. Here are some of the benefits of investing:

Build Wealth

Investing can be a powerful tool to build wealth over time. By investing in stocks, mutual funds, or other financial products, your money has the potential to grow and earn a higher return than traditional savings accounts.

Beat Inflation

Inflation can erode the purchasing power of your money over time. Investing can help you beat inflation by earning a higher return on your money than the rate of inflation.

Diversify Your Portfolio

Investing allows you to diversify your portfolio by investing in a variety of assets, such as stocks, bonds, and real estate. Diversification can help reduce risk by spreading your investments across different asset classes.

Meet Financial Goals

Investing can help you meet your financial goals, whether it's saving for retirement, buying a home, or paying for college. By investing early and consistently, you can grow your wealth and achieve your financial objectives.

How to Start Investing with Little Money

Starting to invest with little money can be daunting, but it's possible. Here are some tips to help you get started:

Set Investment Goals

The first step to investing is to set investment goals. Consider your financial objectives, risk tolerance, and time horizon when setting your goals. It's essential to have a clear idea of what you want to achieve with your investments.

Start Small

Starting small is key to investing on a budget. You don't need a lot of money to start investing. Many investment platforms allow you to start with as little as $10.

Invest Consistently

Investing consistently is more important than investing a large sum of money. Even if you're only investing a small amount each month, the key is to invest consistently over time. This way, your investments can grow through the power of compounding.

Take Advantage of Employer Retirement Plans

If your employer offers a retirement plan, such as a 401(k) or 403(b), take advantage of it. Employer-sponsored retirement plans often offer matching contributions, which is essentially free money. Even if you can only afford to contribute a small amount, it's worth it to take advantage of this benefit.

Low-Cost Investment Options

Investing on a budget doesn't mean sacrificing quality or returns. There are many low-cost investment options available to help you build wealth over time. Here are some of the best low-cost investment options:

Index Funds

Index funds are a type of mutual fund that tracks a particular stock market index, such as the S&P 500. Index funds offer a low-cost way to invest in a diversified portfolio of stocks. They also tend to have lower fees than actively managed funds.

Exchange-Traded Funds (ETFs)

ETFs are similar to index funds, but they trade like individual stocks on an exchange. ETFs are a popular low-cost investment option because they offer instant diversification, low fees, and tax efficiency.

Robo-Advisors

Robo-advisors are digital investment platforms that use algorithms to manage your investments. Robo-advisors offer low fees, automated portfolio management, and access to a diversified portfolio of assets. They are a great option for those who want to invest on a budget but may not have the time or expertise to manage their investments themselves.

Target-Date Funds

Target-date funds are a type of mutual fund that adjusts its asset allocation based on a specific target date, such as retirement.

Target-date funds offer a diversified portfolio of assets that automatically adjust as you get closer to your target date. They also tend to have lower fees than actively managed funds.

Investment Apps

Investment apps, such as Robinhood or Acorns, offer a low-cost way to invest in stocks, ETFs, and other financial products. These apps often have no account minimums and low fees, making them a great option for those starting to invest with little money.

Investing on a budget may seem challenging, but it's possible. By setting investment goals, starting small, and investing consistently, you can build wealth over time. Remember to take advantage of employer retirement plans and explore low-cost investment options such as index funds, ETFs, robo-advisors, target-date funds, and investment apps. With a little research and a long-term investment mindset, you can achieve your financial goals and build a brighter financial future for yourself.

Chapter 13: Planning for Retirement

Retirement is a time of life that many of us look forward to. It's a time when we can finally slow down, spend time with loved ones, and enjoy the fruits of our labor. But to make the most of your retirement, you need to plan ahead. In this chapter, we'll explore retirement savings strategies, the power of compound interest, and how to create a retirement plan on a budget.

Retirement Savings Strategies

Retirement savings strategies are essential for anyone who wants to retire comfortably. Here are some strategies to consider:

Start Early

The earlier you start saving for retirement, the better. Compound interest can work wonders over the long term, so the earlier you start, the more time your investments have to grow. Even if you're starting late, it's never too late to start saving.

Contribute to Retirement Accounts

Retirement accounts, such as 401(k)s and IRAs, offer tax advantages that can help your retirement savings grow faster. Contributions to traditional 401(k)s and IRAs are tax-deductible, meaning you can lower your taxable income while saving for retirement. Roth 401(k)s and IRAs are funded with after-tax dollars, but withdrawals are tax-free in retirement.

Maximize Employer Matching Contributions

If your employer offers a retirement plan with matching contributions, make sure you're taking full advantage of it. Matching contributions are essentially free money, so contribute at least enough to get the maximum match.

Consider Health Savings Accounts (HSAs)

HSAs are tax-advantaged savings accounts that can be used to pay for medical expenses. They also offer retirement savings benefits. Contributions are tax-deductible, earnings grow tax-free, and withdrawals are tax-free when used for qualified medical expenses. Unused funds roll over from year to year and can be used in retirement.

The Power of Compound Interest

Compound interest is the concept of earning interest on top of interest. It's a powerful force that can work wonders for your retirement savings. Here's an example of how compound interest works:

Let's say you invest $10,000 at an annual interest rate of 5%. After one year, you'll have earned $500 in interest, bringing your total to $10,500. If you leave that money in the account and continue to earn 5% interest, after two years, you'll have earned $551.25 in interest, bringing your total to $11,051.25. The longer your money stays invested, the more it can grow through the power of compounding.

Creating a Retirement Plan on a Budget

Creating a retirement plan on a budget may seem challenging, but it's possible. Here are some tips to help you create a retirement plan that works for you:

Determine Your Retirement Goals

The first step in creating a retirement plan is to determine your retirement goals. Consider factors such as when you want to retire, how much income you'll need in retirement, and how much you need to save to reach your goals.

Estimate Your Retirement Income

Estimate your retirement income by looking at sources such as Social Security, pensions, and retirement savings accounts. This will give you an idea of how much income you'll have in retirement.

Calculate Your Retirement Expenses

Calculate your retirement expenses by looking at your current expenses and considering how they may change in retirement. This will give you an idea of how much income you'll need in retirement to maintain your standard of living.

Create a Savings Plan

Create a savings plan that will help you reach your retirement goals. Consider how much you need to save each month and how you'll invest your savings to reach your goals.

Adjust Your Plan as Needed

Your retirement plan should be flexible and able to adapt to changes in your life. Adjust your plan as needed if your financial situation changes or if you need to make adjustments to your retirement goals.

When creating a retirement plan on a budget, it's important to be realistic about your goals and to consider all of your options. You may need to make sacrifices in order to save more money, but the benefits of a secure retirement will be worth it in the end.

Retirement may seem far off, but it's important to start planning for it as soon as possible. With the right retirement savings strategies and a solid plan, you can achieve your retirement goals and enjoy the life you've worked so hard for. Remember, it's never too early or too late to start planning for retirement. The earlier you start, the more time you have to benefit from the power of compound interest, but it's never too late to start saving and investing in your future.

In the end, retirement planning is all about balance. It's about finding the right balance between saving for the future and enjoying the present. It's about setting goals and working towards them, while still enjoying the journey along the way. With careful planning, discipline, and a little bit of luck, you can achieve the retirement of your dreams.

Chapter 14: Shopping on a Budget

Shopping can be a fun and exciting experience, but it can also be a source of stress and financial strain. If you're living on a budget, it's essential to find ways to save money while still enjoying the things you love. In this chapter, we'll explore tips for finding the best deals, strategies for avoiding impulse buys, and making smart purchasing decisions.

Tips for Finding the Best Deals

Finding the best deals takes time and effort, but it's worth it to save money in the long run. Here are some tips to help you find the best deals:

Compare Prices

Comparing prices is one of the easiest ways to save money. Before making a purchase, check the prices at different retailers to make sure you're getting the best deal. There are plenty of price comparison websites and apps that can help you find the best prices.

Shop Online

Shopping online can be a great way to save money. Online retailers often offer lower prices than brick-and-mortar stores, and you can easily compare prices from different websites. Additionally, many online retailers offer free shipping, which can save you even more money.

Use Coupons and Promo Codes

Coupons and promo codes are a great way to save money on your purchases. Before making a purchase, check for coupons and promo codes online. There are plenty of websites that offer coupons and promo codes for various retailers.

Shop Sales and Clearance Sections

Shopping sales and clearance sections can be a great way to save money. Many retailers offer discounts on items that are out of season or overstocked. Additionally, many retailers have sales throughout the year, such as Black Friday and Cyber Monday, which offer significant discounts on a wide range of products.

Buy in Bulk

Buying in bulk can be a great way to save money on certain items, such as non-perishable goods. Many retailers offer discounts for buying in bulk, so if you have the space to store larger quantities of items, it can be a great way to save money in the long run.

Strategies for Avoiding Impulse Buys

Impulse buys can be a significant source of financial strain. Here are some strategies to help you avoid impulse buys:

Make a Shopping List

Making a shopping list is an easy way to avoid impulse buys. Before going shopping, make a list of the items you need, and stick to it. This will help you avoid buying items that you don't need or can't afford.

Set a Budget

Setting a budget is another great way to avoid impulse buys. Before going shopping, decide how much money you can afford to spend, and stick to it. This will help you avoid overspending and buying items you can't afford.

Wait 24 Hours

If you're considering making an impulse buy, wait 24 hours before making the purchase. This will give you time to think about whether or not you really need the item and whether or not you can afford it.

Avoid Sales

Sales can be a great way to save money, but they can also be a source of impulse buys. If you're trying to avoid impulse buys, it's best to avoid sales altogether.

Shop with a Friend

Shopping with a friend can be a great way to avoid impulse buys. Your friend can help keep you accountable and discourage you from making purchases you don't need.

Making Smart Purchasing Decisions

Making smart purchasing decisions is essential when you're living on a budget. Here are some tips to help you make smart purchasing decisions:

Consider the Long-Term Cost

When making a purchase, consider the long-term cost of the item. For example, a cheaper product may seem like a good deal initially, but it may end up costing you more in the long run if it doesn't last as long or requires frequent repairs or replacements. It's important to consider the value of the item and how long it will last before making a purchase.

Read Reviews

Reading reviews from other customers can be a great way to determine if a product is worth purchasing. Many websites have reviews from other customers, which can give you insight into the quality of the product and whether or not it's worth the investment.

Consider Used Items

Consider purchasing used items, such as furniture or electronics, to save money. Used items can often be found at a fraction of the cost of new items, and they can still be in good condition. Just make sure to inspect the item thoroughly before making a purchase.

Ask for Discounts

Don't be afraid to ask for discounts. Many retailers offer discounts to students, military personnel, or other groups. Additionally, some retailers may offer discounts if you pay in cash instead of using a credit card.

Check Return Policies

Before making a purchase, check the retailer's return policy. Make sure you're aware of the return window and any restrictions on returns. This will help you make an informed decision and avoid buying items that you can't return if you're not satisfied with them.

Shopping on a budget can be challenging, but it's not impossible. By following these tips, you can find the best deals, avoid impulse buys, and make smart purchasing decisions. Remember, the key to shopping on a budget is to be mindful of your spending and prioritize your needs over your wants. With a little effort and planning, you can enjoy the things you love without breaking the bank.

Chapter 15: Traveling on a Budget

Traveling is a wonderful way to explore new places, experience different cultures, and create unforgettable memories. However, traveling can also be expensive, and it may seem like an unattainable luxury if you're on a tight budget. But don't despair - with some creativity and planning, it's possible to travel affordably and make your dream of exploring the world a reality. In this chapter, we'll explore tips for traveling on a budget, finding cheap flights and accommodations, and creative ways to explore the world without breaking the bank.

How to Travel Affordably

Traveling on a budget doesn't mean you have to sacrifice the quality of your experience. With some smart planning and resourcefulness, you can travel affordably and still have a great time. Here are some tips to help you travel affordably:

Choose Your Destination Wisely

One of the easiest ways to save money on travel is to choose your destination wisely. Consider traveling to places that are less touristy, as they tend to be less expensive. For example, instead of visiting popular destinations like Paris or New York, consider exploring cities like Budapest or Lisbon. These cities offer plenty of charm and beauty, but are less expensive than their more popular counterparts.

Travel During the Off-Season

Traveling during the off-season can be a great way to save money on your trip. Flights and accommodations tend to be less expensive, and there are usually fewer crowds to contend with. Additionally, traveling during the off-season can give you a chance to experience a destination in a different way, without the hustle and bustle of peak tourist season.

Use Public Transportation

Using public transportation is a great way to save money on travel. Instead of renting a car or taking taxis, consider using buses, trains, or subways to get around. Not only is it less expensive, but it can also give you a chance to experience a destination like a local.

Eat Like a Local

Eating like a local can be a great way to save money on your trip. Instead of dining at expensive restaurants, consider trying street food or local markets. Not only is it less expensive, but it can also give you a chance to experience the local cuisine and culture.

Be Flexible

Being flexible is key to traveling affordably. This means being flexible with your travel dates, destinations, and accommodations. By being flexible, you can take advantage of deals and discounts, and find the best prices for your trip.

Finding Cheap Flights and Accommodations

Flights and accommodations are usually the biggest expenses when it comes to travel. But with some savvy planning, you can find cheap flights and accommodations and save money on your trip. Here are some tips to help you find cheap flights and accommodations:

Use Flight Aggregators

Flight aggregators like Skyscanner or Kayak can be a great way to find cheap flights. These websites allow you to search for flights from multiple airlines, and compare prices to find the best deal. Additionally, many of these websites allow you to set up alerts for price drops or deals, so you can snag a great deal when it becomes available.

Look for Package Deals

Package deals can be a great way to save money on travel. Many airlines and hotels offer package deals that combine flights and accommodations at a discounted rate. Additionally, booking through a travel agent can often result in package deals that can save you money.

Stay in Hostels

Staying in hostels can be a great way to save money on accommodations. Hostels offer shared dormitory-style rooms, which are less expensive than private hotel rooms. Additionally, many hostels offer communal spaces and organized activities, which can be a great way to meet fellow travelers and make new friends.

Consider Alternative Accommodations

If hostels aren't your thing, there are other alternative accommodations that can be less expensive than hotels. For example, Airbnb or Vrbo offer short-term rentals that can be less expensive than traditional hotels. Additionally, camping or staying in a camper van can be a great way to save money on accommodations while experiencing nature.

Book in Advance

Booking in advance can be a great way to save money on flights and accommodations. Many airlines and hotels offer discounted rates for bookings made in advance. Additionally, booking in advance can give you more options and allow you to snag the best deals.

Creative Ways to Explore the World on a Budget

Traveling on a budget doesn't mean you have to stick to a strict itinerary or miss out on unique experiences. In fact, some of the best travel experiences can be had on a shoestring budget. Here are some creative ways to explore the world on a budget:

Volunteer

Volunteering can be a great way to explore the world while giving back. Many organizations offer volunteer programs that include room and board, which can be a great way to save money on accommodations and meals. Additionally, volunteering can give you a chance to learn new skills, meet locals, and make a positive impact on the community.

Take a Road Trip

Taking a road trip can be a great way to explore the world on a budget. With a little planning, you can create a route that includes free or low-cost attractions, campsites, and meals. Additionally, taking a road trip can give you a chance to experience the beauty of the open road and the freedom of traveling on your own terms.

Attend Local Festivals and Events

Attending local festivals and events can be a great way to experience the culture of a destination without breaking the bank. Many festivals and events offer free or low-cost admission, and can give you a chance to see local traditions and customs in action.

Work and Travel

Working while traveling can be a great way to offset the costs of your trip. Many destinations offer work and travel programs that allow you to work in exchange for room and board. Additionally, working remotely or freelancing can give you the flexibility to travel while still earning an income.

Traveling on a budget may require a little extra planning and resourcefulness, but it's possible to explore the world without breaking the bank. By choosing your destination wisely, traveling during the off-season, using public transportation, eating like a local, and being flexible, you can save money on your trip. Additionally, by finding cheap flights and accommodations, and exploring creative ways to travel, you can create unforgettable travel experiences without spending a fortune. So go ahead, start planning your next adventure, and see the world on a budget!

Chapter 16: Managing Debt

Debt can be a heavy burden to bear, both financially and emotionally. Whether it's credit card debt, student loans, or a mortgage, debt can be overwhelming and stressful. However, with some strategies for managing debt and staying on track with payments, it's possible to reduce debt and regain financial freedom. In this chapter, we'll explore tips for managing debt, avoiding debt traps, and staying on track with debt payments.

Strategies for Managing Debt

When it comes to managing debt, there are several strategies you can use to reduce debt and regain financial stability. Here are some tips for managing debt:

Create a Budget

Creating a budget is one of the most important steps in managing debt. A budget can help you see exactly where your money is going, and where you can cut back on expenses. Start by listing all of your monthly income and expenses, including bills, groceries, entertainment, and other expenses. Then, look for areas where you can cut back on expenses, and allocate more money towards debt payments.

Pay More than the Minimum Payment

Paying more than the minimum payment on your debts can help you reduce debt more quickly. This is because the more you pay towards your debt, the less interest you will accrue over time. Look for ways to increase your debt payments, such as cutting back on unnecessary expenses or taking on a side hustle.

Consider Consolidation

Debt consolidation can be a helpful strategy for managing debt. This involves combining multiple debts into one loan, often with a lower interest rate. This can make it easier to manage debt payments and reduce overall debt over time. However, it's important to carefully consider the terms of the consolidation loan, including the interest rate and any fees associated with the loan.

Prioritize High-Interest Debt

If you have multiple debts, prioritize paying off the ones with the highest interest rates first. This is because high-interest debt can accrue more quickly, making it harder to pay off over time. By focusing on high-interest debt first, you can reduce overall debt more quickly and save money on interest charges.

Avoiding Debt Traps

Avoiding debt traps is an important part of managing debt. Debt traps can include high-interest credit cards, payday loans, and other types of loans that can quickly spiral out of control. Here are some tips for avoiding debt traps:

Be Cautious with Credit Cards

Credit cards can be a useful tool for building credit and making purchases. However, it's important to use credit cards responsibly and avoid carrying a balance. This is because credit card interest rates can be high, and carrying a balance can quickly lead to a cycle of debt. If you do use credit cards, be sure to pay them off in full each month.

Avoid Payday Loans

Payday loans can be tempting when you need cash quickly. However, they often come with high interest rates and fees, making them a debt trap. Instead, consider alternatives such as borrowing from family or friends, or taking out a personal loan from a bank or credit union.

Don't Borrow More than You Can Afford

When taking out a loan, it's important to only borrow what you can afford to repay. This means considering your income and expenses, and making sure you have a plan to pay off the loan over time. If you borrow more than you can afford, it can quickly lead to a cycle of debt and financial hardship.

Staying on Track with Debt Payments

Staying on track with debt payments is crucial for reducing debt over time. Here are some tips for staying on track with debt payments:

Set Up Automatic Payments

Setting up automatic payments can be a helpful way to ensure that you never miss a payment. This can help you avoid late fees and keep your credit score in good standing. Many lenders offer automatic payment options, so be sure to check with your lenders to see if this is an option for you.

Make a Payment Plan

Creating a payment plan can help you stay on track with debt payments and make progress towards paying off your debt. Start by listing all of your debts, including the interest rates and minimum payments. Then, determine how much you can realistically afford to pay towards your debts each month. Use this information to create a payment plan that prioritizes high-interest debt and allocates more money towards debt payments over time.

Stay Organized

Staying organized can help you stay on top of your debt payments and avoid missing payments. Keep track of due dates, minimum payments, and balances for all of your debts. This can be done through a spreadsheet, an app, or even a simple notebook. By staying organized, you can ensure that you never miss a payment and stay on track towards debt reduction.

Celebrate Small Wins

Paying off debt can be a long and challenging journey, so it's important to celebrate small wins along the way. This can include paying off a credit card, reaching a debt reduction milestone, or sticking to your budget for a month. Celebrating these small wins can help you stay motivated and focused on your goal of reducing debt.

Managing debt can be a challenging and stressful task, but it's important for achieving financial stability and freedom. By creating a budget, paying more than the minimum payment, considering consolidation, prioritizing high-interest debt, avoiding debt traps, and staying on track with debt payments, you can reduce debt and regain control of your finances. Remember to celebrate small wins along the way and stay focused on your goal of becoming debt-free.

Chapter 17: Building Wealth

Building wealth is a goal that many people aspire to, but few achieve. It requires dedication, hard work, and a mindset that is focused on long-term success. In this chapter, we'll explore the mindset of wealth building, how to build wealth on a budget, and strategies for increasing your net worth.

The Mindset of Wealth Building

Building wealth starts with a mindset that is focused on long-term success. It's about having a clear vision of what you want to achieve and a plan for how you're going to get there. Here are some key mindset shifts to help you build wealth:

Focus on Your Goals

One of the most important mindset shifts for building wealth is to focus on your goals. This means identifying what you want to achieve, setting a plan for how you're going to get there, and staying focused on your goals even when things get tough.

Be Willing to Take Risks

Building wealth often requires taking risks, whether it's starting a business or investing in the stock market. This doesn't mean you should be reckless with your money, but it does mean you should be willing to take calculated risks in pursuit of your goals.

Stay Disciplined

Building wealth requires discipline and self-control. This means sticking to a budget, avoiding unnecessary expenses, and staying focused on your long-term goals even when you're tempted to give up.

Think Long-Term

Building wealth is a marathon, not a sprint. It's about making smart choices today that will pay off in the long run. This means thinking long-term and being willing to delay gratification in pursuit of your goals.

How to Build Wealth on a Budget

Building wealth doesn't necessarily require a large income or a trust fund. It's possible to build wealth on a budget by making smart choices with your money. Here are some tips for building wealth on a budget:

Start by Creating a Budget

The first step in building wealth on a budget is to create a budget. This means tracking your income and expenses, and identifying areas where you can cut back on expenses. Start by listing all of your monthly income and expenses, including bills, groceries, entertainment, and other expenses. Then, look for areas where you can cut back on expenses, and allocate more money towards savings and investments.

Automate Your Savings

One of the best ways to build wealth on a budget is to automate your savings. This means setting up automatic transfers from your checking account to your savings account or investment account. By automating your savings, you'll be more likely to save consistently and build wealth over time.

Focus on Debt Reduction

Debt can be a major barrier to building wealth. It's important to focus on debt reduction as a key part of your wealth building strategy. Start by paying off high-interest debt, such as credit card debt or payday loans. Once you've paid off your high-interest debt, focus on paying off other debts, such as student loans or a mortgage.

Invest in Low-Cost Index Funds

Investing in low-cost index funds is a great way to build wealth on a budget. Index funds are a type of mutual fund that tracks a specific stock market index, such as the S&P 500. They offer low fees and broad exposure to the stock market, making them a great option for long-term investors.

Strategies for Increasing Your Net Worth

Increasing your net worth is a key part of building wealth. Your net worth is the value of your assets (such as your home, investments, and savings) minus your liabilities (such as debt). Here are some strategies for increasing your net worth:

Increase Your Income

Increasing your income is a great way to increase your net worth. This can be done by negotiating a raise at work, starting a side hustle, or investing in your education and skills to qualify for higher-paying jobs. It's important to be strategic and intentional about increasing your income, and to use the extra money to pay down debt or invest in your future.

Reduce Your Expenses

Reducing your expenses is another effective way to increase your net worth. This means cutting back on unnecessary expenses and finding ways to save money on essentials, such as groceries and housing. By reducing your expenses, you'll free up more money to put towards savings and investments.

Invest in Real Estate

Investing in real estate can be a great way to increase your net worth. This can be done by buying rental properties or by investing in real estate investment trusts (REITs). Real estate can provide passive income and can appreciate in value over time, making it a valuable asset in your wealth-building portfolio.

Diversify Your Investments

Diversifying your investments is important for reducing risk and increasing your net worth. This means investing in a mix of stocks, bonds, and other assets to spread out your risk. It's also important to diversify within each asset class, such as investing in a mix of large-cap and small-cap stocks.

Take Advantage of Tax-Advantaged Accounts

Tax-advantaged accounts, such as 401(k)s and IRAs, are powerful tools for building wealth. These accounts offer tax benefits that can help you save more money and increase your net worth over time. Be sure to take advantage of these accounts and contribute as much as you can afford.

Building wealth is a journey that requires patience, discipline, and a long-term perspective. It's important to focus on your goals, be willing to take risks, and stay disciplined in pursuit of your wealth-building goals. By creating a budget, automating your savings, reducing your debt, and investing wisely, you can increase your net worth and achieve financial freedom over time. Remember, wealth-building is a marathon, not a sprint, so stay focused and stay the course.

Chapter 18: Managing Your Time

Time is a precious resource that we all have in equal measure. However, how we use our time can make all the difference in our lives. Effective time management can help us achieve our goals, reduce stress, and increase our overall sense of well-being. In this chapter, we'll explore the importance of time management, strategies for maximizing your time, and balancing work and life on a budget.

The Importance of Time Management

Time management is the process of organizing and planning how much time you spend on different activities. It's about making the most of your time by setting priorities, allocating time for important tasks, and eliminating time-wasting activities. Effective time management has several benefits, including:

Achieving your goals: By managing your time effectively, you can ensure that you're using your time to work towards your goals, whether personal or professional.

Reducing stress: When you manage your time well, you're less likely to feel overwhelmed and stressed out by your workload.

Increasing productivity: Effective time management helps you to be more productive, which can lead to better results and outcomes.

Improving work-life balance: By managing your time effectively, you can ensure that you have time for both work and leisure activities, leading to a better work-life balance.

Strategies for Maximizing Your Time

Effective time management is a skill that can be developed through practice and persistence. Here are some strategies for maximizing your time:

Set Priorities: Identify the most important tasks and activities that you need to accomplish and focus on those first. This will help you to use your time effectively and achieve your goals.

Create a Schedule: Make a schedule that includes time for important tasks, such as work, exercise, and leisure activities. Having a schedule can help you to stay on track and avoid wasting time on unimportant tasks.

Eliminate Distractions: Distractions, such as social media or email notifications, can be a major time-waster. Try to eliminate distractions by turning off notifications or using an app to block distracting websites during work hours.

Learn to Say No: Saying yes to every request can leave you feeling overwhelmed and stressed. Learn to say no to requests that don't align with your priorities or goals.

Take Breaks: Taking regular breaks can help you to stay focused and productive. Try taking a short walk or stretching every hour to keep your energy levels up.

Balancing Work and Life on a Budget

Balancing work and life can be challenging, especially when you're on a budget. Here are some tips for balancing work and life on a budget:

Create a Budget: Creating a budget can help you to manage your finances and ensure that you have enough money for both work-related expenses and leisure activities.

Prioritize Leisure Activities: Make leisure activities a priority by scheduling them into your calendar and budgeting for them accordingly. This will help you to maintain a good work-life balance and reduce stress.

Look for Low-Cost Activities: There are many low-cost or free leisure activities, such as hiking, biking, or reading. Look for activities that you enjoy and that don't require a lot of money.

Make Use of Your Lunch Break: Use your lunch break to take a walk, read a book, or engage in another leisure activity. This can help you to recharge and reduce stress during the workday.

Set Boundaries: Set boundaries between work and leisure time by avoiding checking work email or taking work calls outside of work hours. This will help you to maintain a healthy work-life balance and reduce stress.

Effective time management is essential for achieving your goals, reducing stress, and improving your overall sense of well-being. By setting priorities, creating a schedule, eliminating distractions, learning to say no, and taking breaks, you can maximize your time and be more productive. Balancing work and life on a budget is also important, and can be achieved by creating a budget, prioritizing leisure activities, looking for low-cost activities, making use of your lunch break, and setting boundaries. Remember, time is a precious resource that can't be replaced, so use it wisely and make the most of every moment.

Chapter 19: Building a Support Network

Life can be challenging, and we all face times when we need help and support. Having a strong support network can make all the difference during these difficult times. In this chapter, we'll explore why a support network is important, how to build one, and where to find help when you need it.

Why a Support Network is Important

A support network is a group of people who provide emotional, practical, and sometimes financial support during challenging times. Whether you're facing a difficult life event, struggling with a mental health issue, or simply need someone to talk to, having a support network can make all the difference.

Here are some reasons why a support network is important:

Emotional Support: A support network can provide emotional support during difficult times. Whether you need a listening ear or a shoulder to cry on, having someone to turn to can help you feel less alone.

Practical Support: A support network can also provide practical support, such as helping you move house or providing childcare during a busy time. Having people who are willing to help can make all the difference in managing life's challenges.

Perspective and Advice: A support network can provide different perspectives and advice when you're facing a difficult decision or situation. This can help you see things from a different angle and make more informed choices.

Increased Resilience: Having a support network can increase your resilience during challenging times. When you know you have people who care about you and are willing to help, you're better able to bounce back from difficult situations.

How to Build a Support Network

Building a support network takes time and effort, but it's worth it in the long run. Here are some tips for building a support network:

Identify Your Needs: Start by identifying your needs and the types of support that would be helpful to you. Do you need emotional support, practical help, or someone to talk to? Knowing what you need can help you find the right people to support you.

Reach Out to Friends and Family: Friends and family are often the first people we turn to for support. Reach out to the people in your life who you trust and feel comfortable talking to. Let them know what you're going through and how they can help.

Join a Support Group: Support groups are a great way to connect with others who are going through similar experiences. Whether you're dealing with a health condition, addiction, or grief, there are support groups out there for almost any situation.

Volunteer: Volunteering is a great way to meet new people and build connections. Look for volunteer opportunities in your community that align with your interests and values.

Attend Events and Meetups: Attend events and meetups in your community that align with your interests. Whether it's a book club, a yoga class, or a cooking class, these events are a great way to meet new people and build connections.

Finding Help When You Need It

Sometimes, despite our best efforts, we need help beyond our support network. Here are some resources for finding help when you need it:

Mental Health Services: If you're struggling with a mental health issue, there are many resources available to you. Look for mental health services in your community, such as counseling or therapy.

Hotlines: Hotlines are available for a variety of issues, including mental health, domestic violence, and substance abuse. These hotlines provide free, confidential support and advice.

Community Services: Look for community services in your area that provide support and assistance. These services may include food banks, housing assistance, and job training.

Online Communities: There are many online communities that provide support and advice for a variety of issues. Look for online communities that align with your interests and needs, such as mental health forums or support groups for specific health conditions.

Here are some additional tips for finding help when you need it:

Don't Be Afraid to Ask: It can be difficult to ask for help, but it's important to remember that it's okay to ask. Don't be afraid to reach out to friends, family, or professional resources when you need help.

Research Your Options: Take the time to research your options for support and assistance. This can include looking online, asking for recommendations from trusted sources, and reaching out to community organizations.

Be Persistent: Finding the right support and assistance can take time and effort. Don't give up if you don't find the right fit right away. Keep reaching out and exploring your options until you find the right support for your needs.

Building a support network is an important part of navigating life's challenges. Whether you're facing a difficult life event or simply need someone to talk to, having people in your life who provide emotional, practical, and sometimes financial support can make all the difference. By identifying your needs, reaching out to friends and family, joining support groups, volunteering, and attending events and meetups, you can build a strong support network that can help you during difficult times. And if you need additional help, don't hesitate to reach out to professional resources or community services. Remember, you don't have to go through difficult times alone.

Chapter 20: Building a Better Future

We all have dreams and aspirations for our future, but it can be hard to know where to start when it comes to making them a reality. In this chapter, we'll explore how extreme budgeting can change your life, creating a vision for your future, and staying motivated and committed to building a better future for yourself.

How Extreme Budgeting Can Change Your Life

One of the most important things you can do to build a better future for yourself is to get your finances in order. Extreme budgeting is a way to take control of your finances and make every dollar count. It's about cutting out unnecessary expenses and prioritizing your spending to align with your goals and values.

Here are some tips for extreme budgeting:

Track Your Spending: Start by tracking your spending for a month. Write down everything you spend money on, no matter how small. This will give you a clear picture of where your money is going and where you can make cuts.

Create a Budget: Once you've tracked your spending, create a budget. List all of your income and expenses and prioritize your spending. Make sure your spending aligns with your goals and values.

Cut Expenses: Look for ways to cut expenses. Cancel subscriptions you don't use, buy generic brands, and cook at home instead of eating out. Every dollar you save can be put toward your future goals.

Pay Off Debt: If you have debt, make paying it off a priority. Debt can be a major roadblock to building a better future. Look for ways to pay off debt quickly, such as using the debt snowball method.

Invest in Your Future: Make sure you're investing in your future. This could mean contributing to a retirement account, starting a side hustle, or going back to school to learn a new skill.

Creating a Vision for Your Future

Once you have your finances in order, it's time to create a vision for your future. What do you want to achieve? What kind of life do you want to live? Creating a vision for your future can help you stay motivated and committed to building a better future for yourself.

Here are some tips for creating a vision for your future:

Reflect on Your Values: Start by reflecting on your values. What's important to you? What kind of life do you want to live? Use your values to guide your vision for the future.

Visualize Your Future: Take some time to visualize your future. What does it look like? Where are you living? What kind of work are you doing? Visualizing your future can help make it feel more real and achievable.

Set Goals: Break down your vision for the future into smaller, achievable goals. Write them down and create a plan to achieve them. Celebrate your successes along the way.

Stay Positive: Building a better future takes time and effort. Stay positive and focused on your goals. Don't let setbacks derail you. Keep moving forward.

Staying Motivated and Committed

Staying motivated and committed to building a better future can be challenging. Life is full of distractions and obstacles. Here are some tips for staying motivated and committed:

Find a Support System: Surround yourself with people who support your goals and values. Lean on them when you need encouragement or advice.

Stay Accountable: Hold yourself accountable for achieving your goals. Share your goals with others and track your progress.

Celebrate Your Successes: Take time to celebrate your successes along the way. This can help keep you motivated and committed.

Stay Focused: Keep your vision for the future in mind and stay focused on your goals. Don't let distractions derail you.

Take Care of Yourself: Building a better future takes time and effort. Make sure you're taking care of yourself along the way. Eat well, exercise, and get enough rest.

Building a better future for yourself is possible, but it takes effort, motivation, and commitment. By implementing extreme budgeting, creating a vision for your future, and staying motivated and committed, you can achieve your goals and live the life you want.

Remember, it's never too late to start. You can start today, no matter where you are in life. Take the first step, track your spending, create a budget, and start setting achievable goals. Celebrate your successes along the way, and don't let setbacks derail you.

With dedication and hard work, you can build a better future for yourself. Keep your vision in mind, stay motivated, and stay committed. Your future is in your hands, and you have the power to make it a reality.

Chapter 21: Overcoming Obstacles

Building a better future through extreme budgeting is not an easy task. Along the way, you will face many obstacles that can derail your progress. These obstacles can be financial, emotional, or mental, and it's important to know how to overcome them to stay on track.

In this chapter, we'll explore some common obstacles to extreme budgeting, strategies for overcoming them, and tips for staying motivated through challenges.

Common Obstacles to Extreme Budgeting

Unexpected Expenses: One of the most common obstacles to extreme budgeting is unexpected expenses. These could be car repairs, medical bills, or home repairs. These expenses can throw off your budget and make it difficult to save for the future.

Emotional Spending: Emotional spending is another common obstacle to extreme budgeting. This could be retail therapy after a bad day at work or buying things you don't need because you feel stressed or anxious.

Peer Pressure: Peer pressure can also be an obstacle to extreme budgeting. It's easy to get caught up in trying to keep up with friends or colleagues who have a higher standard of living. This can lead to overspending and difficulty sticking to your budget.

Lack of Discipline: Lack of discipline is another common obstacle to extreme budgeting. It can be hard to resist temptation and stick to your budget when you're faced with things you want but don't necessarily need.

Strategies for Overcoming Obstacles

Emergency Fund: To overcome unexpected expenses, it's important to have an emergency fund. This is a savings account specifically for unexpected expenses. Aim to have at least three to six months' worth of expenses saved in this account.

Mindful Spending: To overcome emotional spending, practice mindful spending. Before making a purchase, ask yourself if it's something you really need or if you're just buying it to feel better. If it's the latter, consider other ways to manage your emotions that don't involve spending money.

Set Boundaries: To overcome peer pressure, set boundaries with friends and colleagues. Let them know that you're on a budget and can't afford certain things. You can also suggest alternative activities that are less expensive.

Self-Discipline: To overcome lack of discipline, practice self-discipline. Start small by cutting out one unnecessary expense a week and gradually increase from there. Use positive affirmations to reinforce your commitment to extreme budgeting.

Staying Motivated Through Challenges

Staying motivated through challenges is key to overcoming obstacles and achieving your goals. Here are some tips for staying motivated:

Visualize Your Goals: Keep your goals in mind by visualizing them regularly. Imagine yourself achieving your goals and how it will feel. This can help you stay motivated during tough times.

Break Down Your Goals: Break down your goals into smaller, achievable steps. This will help you see progress and stay motivated.

Find Support: Find support from family and friends who are also committed to extreme budgeting. Join online communities or attend in-person meetings to connect with like-minded individuals.

Celebrate Successes: Celebrate your successes, no matter how small. This can help you stay motivated and reinforce your commitment to extreme budgeting.

Learn From Setbacks: Don't let setbacks derail you. Instead, learn from them and use them as an opportunity to grow and improve.

Take Care of Yourself: Building a better future through extreme budgeting can be stressful. Make sure you're taking care of yourself by getting enough sleep, eating well, and taking breaks when needed.

Extreme budgeting is a powerful tool for building a better future, but it's not always easy. Obstacles such as unexpected expenses, emotional spending, peer pressure, and lack of discipline can make it challenging to stick to your budget and achieve your goals. However, by implementing strategies such as building an emergency fund, practicing mindful spending, setting boundaries, and practicing self-discipline, you can overcome these obstacles and stay on track.

It's also important to stay motivated through challenges by visualizing your goals, breaking them down into smaller steps, finding support, celebrating successes, learning from setbacks, and taking care of yourself. By doing so, you can build a better future and achieve financial freedom.

Chapter 22: Creating a Plan for Success

When it comes to achieving any goal, whether it's financial or personal, the power of planning cannot be overstated. Without a plan, it's easy to get off track and lose sight of your goals. However, with a well-thought-out plan, you can stay focused and motivated, even in the face of obstacles.

In this chapter, we'll explore the power of planning, strategies for creating a successful plan, and tips for staying focused on your goals.

The Power of Planning

Planning is the foundation for success. It's what sets successful people apart from those who struggle to achieve their goals. With a plan, you have a roadmap that guides you toward your destination. It helps you stay focused, motivated, and on track, even when faced with obstacles.

Planning also helps you anticipate potential obstacles and develop strategies for overcoming them. It's like a safety net that helps you stay on course, even when things don't go as planned.

Without a plan, it's easy to get sidetracked by distractions, lose sight of your goals, and become overwhelmed. Planning is like a compass that helps you stay on course, even when the winds of life threaten to blow you off course.

Strategies for Creating a Successful Plan

Creating a successful plan requires a bit of effort, but the results are worth it. Here are some strategies for creating a plan that will help you achieve your goals:

Set Clear Goals: The first step in creating a successful plan is to set clear, specific, and achievable goals. Your goals should be measurable, so you can track your progress and adjust your plan as needed. For example, if your goal is to save $10,000 in a year, break it down into smaller, achievable steps, such as saving $833 per month.

Identify Obstacles: Identify potential obstacles that may prevent you from achieving your goals. This could be unexpected expenses, lack of discipline, or external factors such as job loss or illness. Once you've identified potential obstacles, develop strategies for overcoming them.

Create a Budget: A budget is a key component of any successful plan. It helps you track your expenses, identify areas where you can cut back, and ensure you're staying on track toward your financial goals. Use a budgeting app or spreadsheet to track your expenses and adjust your budget as needed.

Develop a Timeline: Developing a timeline is essential for staying on track toward your goals. Break your goals down into smaller steps and assign deadlines to each one. This will help you stay focused and motivated, as well as track your progress.

Accountability: Having someone hold you accountable can be a powerful motivator. Share your goals with a friend or family member and ask them to check in with you regularly. You can also join an accountability group or hire a coach to help keep you on track.

Staying Focused on Your Goals

Creating a successful plan is just the first step. Staying focused on your goals is equally important. Here are some tips for staying focused and motivated:

Keep Your Goals in Mind: Keep your goals in mind by visualizing them regularly. Write them down and display them somewhere you'll see them every day, such as on your bathroom mirror or computer screen.

This will help you stay focused and motivated, even during challenging times.

Celebrate Small Wins: Celebrate your successes, no matter how small. Each small win is a step toward achieving your larger goal. Celebrating your successes will help you stay motivated and reinforce your commitment to achieving your goals.

Stay Positive: A positive mindset is essential for success. Instead of focusing on what you haven't achieved, focus on what you have achieved and the progress you've made. Use positive affirmations to reinforce your commitment to your goals.

Stay Organized: Staying organized is key to staying focused. Keep track of your progress and deadlines, and stay on top of your budget. Use a planner or digital tool to help you stay organized and avoid feeling overwhelmed.

Avoid Distractions: Identify distractions that may be keeping you from achieving your goals, such as social media or TV, and take steps to reduce or eliminate them. Consider setting aside specific times for these activities or using apps that limit your access to them.

Get Support: Surround yourself with people who support your goals and encourage you. Join a community or support group related to your goal, and share your progress and challenges with others.

Creating a plan for success is essential for achieving any goal. It helps you stay focused, motivated, and on track, even when faced with obstacles. By setting clear goals, identifying potential obstacles, developing a budget and timeline, and staying focused and organized, you can achieve your goals and create the life you desire.

Remember, success is not just about achieving your goals; it's also about the journey. Celebrate your successes, learn from your failures, and continue to grow and evolve. With a well-thought-out plan and the right mindset, you can achieve anything you set your mind to.

Chapter 23: Embracing Frugality

In today's world, it's easy to fall into the trap of consumerism. Everywhere we turn, we're bombarded with ads and messages telling us we need the latest gadgets, designer clothes, and luxury cars to be happy and successful. But the truth is, material possessions don't bring lasting happiness or fulfillment. In fact, they can often be a source of stress and anxiety.

That's where frugality comes in. Frugality is about living a simple, sustainable, and intentional life. It's about making conscious choices that align with your values, rather than blindly following societal norms or trying to keep up with the Joneses. In this chapter, we'll explore why frugality is important, strategies for embracing a frugal lifestyle, and tips for finding joy in living on less.

Why Frugality is Important

Frugality is important for several reasons. First, it helps us live within our means and avoid debt. When we live frugally, we prioritize our needs over our wants, and we're less likely to overspend or accumulate unnecessary debt. This can lead to a greater sense of financial security and freedom.

Second, frugality helps us reduce our environmental impact. When we consume less, we reduce our carbon footprint and minimize the resources we consume. This is especially important in today's world, where climate change and environmental degradation are major global challenges.

Third, frugality can help us cultivate gratitude and contentment. When we focus on what we have, rather than what we lack, we're more likely to appreciate the simple pleasures in life and find joy in the present moment. This can lead to a greater sense of happiness and fulfillment.

Strategies for Embracing a Frugal Lifestyle

Embracing a frugal lifestyle doesn't mean sacrificing quality or happiness. It simply means making intentional choices that align with your values and priorities. Here are some strategies for embracing a frugal lifestyle:

Create a Budget: The first step in embracing a frugal lifestyle is to create a budget. This will help you track your income and expenses, identify areas where you can cut back, and set financial goals. Use a budgeting app or spreadsheet to track your expenses and adjust your budget as needed.

Prioritize Your Spending: Prioritize your spending based on your values and priorities. Focus on the things that bring you the most joy and fulfillment, and cut back on the things that don't. For example, if travel is a priority for you, allocate more of your budget to travel and less to dining out or entertainment.

Practice Mindful Consumption: Before making a purchase, ask yourself if it aligns with your values and priorities. Do you really need it, or is it just a temporary impulse? Can you find a more sustainable or affordable alternative? Practicing mindful consumption can help you avoid unnecessary purchases and reduce your environmental impact.

Simplify Your Life: Simplifying your life can help you reduce stress and increase your sense of contentment. This could mean decluttering your home, reducing your social media usage, or cutting back on commitments that don't bring you joy.

Embrace Minimalism: Minimalism is about living with less and focusing on the things that truly matter. It's not about deprivation or asceticism, but about finding joy in simplicity. Embracing minimalism can help you prioritize your values, reduce your environmental impact, and cultivate gratitude and contentment.

Finding Joy in Living on Less

Living on less doesn't have to be a sacrifice. In fact, it can be a source of joy and fulfillment. Here are some tips for finding joy in living on less:

Practice Gratitude: Cultivate gratitude by focusing on the things you do have, rather than the things you don't. Make a habit of expressing gratitude each day for the simple things in your life, like a warm meal, a roof over your head, or a kind gesture from a friend. Gratitude helps us appreciate what we have and find joy in the present moment.

Discover Simple Pleasures: Simple pleasures are often the most meaningful. Take a walk in nature, enjoy a home-cooked meal with loved ones, or curl up with a good book. These activities don't require a lot of money or material possessions, but they can bring a lot of joy and contentment.

Focus on Experiences: Instead of accumulating more stuff, focus on accumulating experiences. Travel to new places, try new hobbies, or spend time with loved ones. Experiences create memories that last a lifetime, and they often bring more joy and fulfillment than material possessions.

Connect with Others: Frugality doesn't have to mean isolation. Connect with others who share your values and interests. Join a community group, volunteer, or participate in a shared hobby. These connections can provide a sense of belonging and fulfillment.

Embrace Creativity: Living frugally often requires creativity. Find ways to repurpose items, create DIY projects, or find affordable alternatives to expensive products. Embracing creativity can be a fun and rewarding way to live on less.

Frugality is about living a simple, sustainable, and intentional life. It's not about sacrificing happiness or quality, but about finding joy and fulfillment in the things that truly matter. By prioritizing our values, practicing mindful consumption, and finding joy in living on less, we can create a more fulfilling and sustainable life.

As a book writer expert, I encourage you to take the time to reflect on your own values and priorities. Ask yourself what truly brings you joy and fulfillment, and how you can align your actions with those values. Embracing frugality can be a powerful way to live a more intentional and fulfilling life, and to make a positive impact on the world around us.

Chapter 24: Creating a Mindset of Abundance

Do you ever feel like there's never enough? Not enough time, not enough money, not enough love? Do you worry about scarcity and struggle to see the abundance in your life? If so, you're not alone. Many of us have been conditioned to think in terms of scarcity, to believe that there's a limited amount of resources in the world, and that we have to fight for our share. But what if we shifted our mindset from scarcity to abundance? What if we believed that there's more than enough to go around, and that we can attract abundance into our lives? In this chapter, we'll explore the abundance mindset, strategies for overcoming scarcity thinking, and tips for attracting abundance into your life.

The Abundance Mindset

The abundance mindset is a way of thinking that focuses on the limitless possibilities and opportunities available in the world. It's about believing that there's more than enough to go around, and that we can all achieve our dreams and goals. This mindset is characterized by positivity, gratitude, and a sense of empowerment.

When we adopt an abundance mindset, we shift our focus from scarcity to abundance. Instead of worrying about what we don't have, we appreciate what we do have and look for opportunities to create more. We focus on our strengths, our passions, and our values, and we use them to create a life that we love.

Overcoming Scarcity Thinking

To create an abundance mindset, we need to overcome scarcity thinking. Scarcity thinking is a way of thinking that focuses on what we don't have, rather than what we do have. It's characterized by negativity, fear, and a sense of lack.

Here are some strategies for overcoming scarcity thinking:

Practice Gratitude: Gratitude is a powerful antidote to scarcity thinking. When we focus on what we're grateful for, we shift our focus from what we don't have to what we do have. Make a habit of practicing gratitude daily, by writing in a gratitude journal or taking a moment to reflect on what you're thankful for.

Challenge Your Beliefs: Scarcity thinking is often rooted in our beliefs about ourselves and the world. Challenge these beliefs by asking yourself if they're really true. Are you really limited in what you can achieve, or are you capable of more than you think?

Focus on Abundance: Focus on the abundance in your life, rather than the scarcity. Look for opportunities to create more abundance, whether it's through your work, your relationships, or your hobbies. Focus on what you can do, rather than what you can't do.

Attracting Abundance into Your Life

Once you've adopted an abundance mindset and overcome scarcity thinking, it's time to start attracting abundance into your life. Here are some tips for attracting abundance:

Set Intentions: Set clear intentions for what you want to attract into your life. Be specific about your goals and visualize yourself already having achieved them. This will help you focus your energy and attract what you want.

Take Action: Attracting abundance requires action. Take steps towards your goals, even if they're small. Every action you take will bring you closer to your dreams.

Be Open: Be open to new opportunities and experiences. Sometimes, abundance comes in unexpected ways. Stay open to the possibilities and be willing to take risks.

Trust the Universe: Trust that the universe is conspiring to bring you what you want. Believe that everything is working out for your highest good, even if it doesn't seem that way at first.

Creating a mindset of abundance takes practice, but it's worth it. When we focus on abundance, we attract more abundance into our lives. We see opportunities where we once saw obstacles, and we create a life that's rich in meaning and purpose. Remember, abundance isn't just about material possessions, it's about a sense of fulfillment and happiness.

So, start today by adopting an abundance mindset, challenging your scarcity thinking, and taking action towards your goals. Trust that the universe has your back and that you have the power to create a life filled with abundance. And always remember to practice gratitude, for the abundance that's already in your life.

The journey towards creating a mindset of abundance is not always easy, but it is always rewarding. When we shift our focus from scarcity to abundance, we open ourselves up to a world of possibilities and opportunities. By practicing gratitude, challenging our beliefs, and taking action towards our goals, we can attract more abundance into our lives. Remember, abundance is not just about having more, it's about being more. So, take the first step towards abundance today and see the magic that unfolds in your life.

Chapter 25: Achieving Financial Freedom

Money is a topic that can bring up a lot of emotions. It's something we all need to live, but it can also cause stress and anxiety. Many of us dream of achieving financial freedom, but the road to get there can feel overwhelming. In this chapter, we'll explore strategies for achieving financial independence, creating a plan for financial freedom, and the mindset shifts necessary to make it a reality.

The Road to Financial Freedom

Financial freedom means having enough passive income to cover your expenses, without the need for a traditional 9-5 job. It's the ability to live life on your own terms, without being tied to a specific income source. Achieving financial freedom is a journey, and it requires a combination of mindset shifts, smart financial decisions, and disciplined saving and investing.

The first step towards financial freedom is understanding your current financial situation. This means taking a deep dive into your income, expenses, debts, and assets. It's important to be honest with yourself about where you stand financially, so you can create a plan to move forward.

The next step is to create a budget and stick to it. A budget is a tool for managing your money and ensuring that you're not overspending or living beyond your means. It's important to track your expenses and income, and adjust your budget as necessary. This will help you identify areas where you can cut back and save more money.

Once you have a budget in place, it's time to focus on paying off debt. High-interest debt, such as credit card debt, can be a major obstacle to achieving financial freedom. It's important to prioritize paying off these debts, and to avoid taking on new debt whenever possible.

Strategies for Achieving Financial Independence

There are several strategies for achieving financial independence. Here are a few key ones to consider:

Save More: Saving more money is a key component of achieving financial freedom. Aim to save at least 20% of your income each month, and consider automating your savings to make it easier.

Invest Wisely: Investing your money can help it grow over time, and increase your passive income streams. Consider working with a financial advisor to create an investment strategy that aligns with your goals and risk tolerance.

Generate Passive Income: Passive income is income that you earn without actively working for it. This can include rental income, dividends from stocks, or income from a business that you own but do not actively run. Building passive income streams is an important part of achieving financial freedom.

Live Below Your Means: Living below your means is essential for achieving financial freedom. This means being intentional about your spending, and avoiding lifestyle inflation. Instead of upgrading your lifestyle every time you get a raise, focus on saving and investing more.

Creating a Plan for Achieving Financial Freedom

Creating a plan for achieving financial freedom requires a combination of goal-setting, budgeting, and investing. Here are some steps to consider when creating your plan:

Set Financial Goals: Set specific, measurable financial goals for yourself. This could include paying off debt, saving for retirement, or building passive income streams.

Create a Budget: Create a budget that aligns with your financial goals. Be realistic about your expenses and income, and prioritize saving and investing.

Pay off Debt: Prioritize paying off high-interest debt, such as credit card debt. Consider using the debt snowball or debt avalanche method to pay off multiple debts at once.

Build an Emergency Fund: Building an emergency fund is essential for financial stability. Aim to save at least 3-6 months' worth of expenses in an emergency fund.

Invest Wisely: Work with a financial advisor to create an investment strategy that aligns with your goals and risk tolerance. Consider diversifying your investments to minimize risk and maximize potential returns.

Build Passive Income Streams: Identify opportunities to build passive income streams, such as investing in rental properties or dividend-paying stocks. This will help you create additional income streams that can supplement your regular income.

Monitor and Adjust: Keep a close eye on your finances and adjust your plan as necessary. Regularly review your budget, investments, and progress towards your financial goals. This will help you stay on track and make adjustments as needed.

The Mindset Shifts Necessary for Financial Freedom

Achieving financial freedom requires more than just financial planning and smart decisions. It also requires a shift in mindset. Here are some mindset shifts to consider:

Embrace Frugality: Embracing frugality means being intentional about your spending and avoiding unnecessary expenses. This can be difficult at first, but it's an essential part of achieving financial freedom.

Focus on the Long-Term: Financial freedom is a long-term goal, and it requires patience and persistence. Focus on the big picture, and don't get discouraged by setbacks or slow progress.

Take Calculated Risks: Building wealth often requires taking risks, but it's important to take calculated risks. This means doing your research and making informed decisions.

Avoid Comparison: Comparing yourself to others can be a major obstacle to achieving financial freedom. Instead, focus on your own progress and goals.

Be Grateful: Practicing gratitude can help shift your mindset towards abundance and away from scarcity. Focus on what you have, rather than what you lack.

Achieving financial freedom is a journey, and it requires a combination of mindset shifts, smart financial decisions, and disciplined saving and investing. It's important to take a deep dive into your current financial situation, create a budget, pay off debt, save more, invest wisely, and build passive income streams. Along the way, it's important to shift your mindset towards frugality, patience, calculated risk-taking, and gratitude. By taking these steps and making these mindset shifts, you can achieve financial freedom and live life on your own terms.

Chapter 26: Maintaining Your Budget

Creating a budget is an essential part of financial planning. It's a tool that helps you manage your money, track your expenses, and achieve your financial goals. But creating a budget is only half the battle. The real challenge is sticking to it over time. In this chapter, we'll explore the importance of maintaining your budget, strategies for sticking to it, and adjusting your budget as necessary.

The Importance of Maintaining Your Budget

Maintaining your budget is crucial for achieving financial stability and freedom. It's the difference between staying on track with your financial goals or falling off course. When you stick to your budget, you're able to manage your expenses, save for the future, and avoid unnecessary debt. It also helps you stay mindful of your spending habits and encourages you to make smarter financial decisions.

On the other hand, failing to maintain your budget can lead to overspending, missed payments, and mounting debt. It can also derail your progress towards financial goals and make it harder to achieve financial freedom.

Strategies for Sticking to Your Budget

Sticking to your budget requires discipline and commitment. Here are some strategies for staying on track:

Track Your Expenses: Keeping track of your expenses is essential for maintaining your budget. It helps you identify areas where you can cut back and stay accountable to your spending habits. You can use budgeting apps or spreadsheets to track your expenses and monitor your progress.

Set Realistic Goals: Setting realistic goals for your budget is important for staying motivated and avoiding burnout. Instead of aiming for drastic changes overnight, focus on small, incremental changes that are achievable.

Use Cash: Using cash instead of credit cards or debit cards can help you stay within your budget. It's easy to overspend when using cards, but when you use cash, you're forced to be more mindful of your purchases.

Avoid Temptations: Avoiding temptations is another key strategy for sticking to your budget. This might mean unsubscribing from shopping emails, avoiding online shopping, or staying away from stores where you're likely to overspend.

Celebrate Small Wins: Celebrating small wins is an important part of staying motivated and committed to your budget. Whether it's reaching a savings goal or sticking to your budget for a week, take time to acknowledge and celebrate your achievements.

Adjusting Your Budget as Necessary

No budget is perfect, and it's normal to need to make adjustments over time. Life is unpredictable, and unexpected expenses can pop up at any time. Here are some tips for adjusting your budget as necessary:

Review Your Budget Regularly: Reviewing your budget regularly helps you stay on top of your finances and identify areas where you may need to adjust. Set aside time each month to review your budget and make any necessary changes.

Prioritize Your Expenses: If unexpected expenses come up, it's important to prioritize your expenses. This means focusing on your essential expenses, such as housing, food, and utilities, and cutting back on non-essential expenses, such as entertainment or dining out.

Be Realistic: When making adjustments to your budget, be realistic about your financial situation. It's important to balance your financial goals with your current income and expenses. Don't set unrealistic expectations that will lead to burnout or frustration.

Stay Positive: Staying positive and focused on your financial goals is key to maintaining your budget over time. Don't let setbacks or unexpected expenses derail your progress. Instead, stay committed to your goals and adjust your budget as necessary.

Maintaining your budget is essential for achieving financial stability and freedom. It requires discipline, commitment, and a willingness to adjust as necessary. By tracking your expenses, setting realistic goals, avoiding temptations, and prioritizing your expenses, you can stick to your budget and achieve your financial goals. Remember, maintaining your budget is not just about limiting your spending; it's about creating a sustainable financial plan that allows you to live within your means while working towards your long-term financial goals.

One important aspect of budgeting that often gets overlooked is the emotional toll it can take. For many people, money is a source of stress and anxiety. Budgeting can amplify these feelings, especially if you're struggling to make ends meet or if unexpected expenses arise.

If you're finding it challenging to stick to your budget, it's important to take care of your emotional well-being as well. Here are some tips for managing the emotional side of budgeting:

Practice Self-Care: Take time to do things that bring you joy and help you relax. This could be anything from reading a book to taking a yoga class. When you prioritize self-care, you're better able to manage stress and anxiety.

Talk to Someone: Don't be afraid to reach out to a friend or family member for support. Talking about your financial struggles can help alleviate stress and anxiety and provide a fresh perspective on your situation.

Focus on Your Progress: Celebrate your progress, no matter how small. Recognize the effort and discipline it takes to stick to a budget and give yourself credit for your accomplishments.

Stay Flexible: Remember that your budget is not set in stone. If unexpected expenses arise, don't beat yourself up for needing to adjust your budget. Stay flexible and make changes as necessary.

Remember Your Why: Finally, keep in mind why you're budgeting in the first place. Whether it's to save for a down payment on a house, pay off debt, or achieve financial independence, reminding yourself of your goals can help you stay motivated and committed to your budget.

Maintaining your budget is an ongoing process that requires patience, discipline, and flexibility. By using the strategies outlined in this chapter and taking care of your emotional well-being, you can create a sustainable financial plan that allows you to achieve your long-term financial goals. Remember, the key to success is staying committed, staying positive, and staying focused on your why.

Chapter 27: Building a Sustainable Lifestyle

As we become increasingly aware of the impact of our actions on the planet, many of us are striving to live a more sustainable lifestyle. But what does that mean, and how can we achieve it without breaking the bank? In this chapter, we'll explore ways to live sustainably on a budget, reduce waste and conserve resources, and find eco-friendly solutions for everyday life.

Living Sustainably on a Budget

Many people assume that living sustainably is expensive, but it doesn't have to be. In fact, living sustainably can actually save you money in the long run. Here are some ways to live sustainably on a budget:

Reduce your energy consumption: One of the easiest ways to live sustainably on a budget is to reduce your energy consumption. Turn off lights when you leave a room, unplug electronics when they're not in use, and switch to energy-efficient appliances.

Use public transportation or walk/cycle: Using public transportation or walking/cycling instead of driving can reduce your carbon footprint and save you money on gas and parking.

Eat less meat: Eating less meat or becoming a vegetarian/vegan is a great way to reduce your environmental impact and save money on groceries.

Buy secondhand: Buying secondhand clothes and furniture is a great way to reduce waste and save money.

Use reusable bags, water bottles, and containers: Using reusable bags, water bottles, and containers is an easy way to reduce waste and save money over time.

Reducing Waste and Conserving Resources

Reducing waste and conserving resources are two essential components of living sustainably. Here are some ways to reduce waste and conserve resources:

Reduce plastic usage: Plastic is a major contributor to waste and pollution. Reduce your plastic usage by using reusable bags, water bottles, and containers, and avoiding single-use plastics like straws and utensils.

Compost: Composting food waste is an easy way to reduce waste and create nutrient-rich soil for your garden.

Buy in bulk: Buying in bulk reduces packaging waste and can save you money over time.

Repair instead of replacing: When something breaks, consider repairing it instead of replacing it. This reduces waste and saves you money.

Use eco-friendly cleaning products: Many conventional cleaning products contain harmful chemicals that are bad for the environment and your health. Switch to eco-friendly cleaning products that are safe and effective.

Finding Eco-Friendly Solutions

There are many eco-friendly solutions for everyday life that can help reduce your environmental impact. Here are some examples:

Use solar power: Installing solar panels is a great way to reduce your carbon footprint and save money on energy bills.

Plant a garden: Growing your own food reduces the environmental impact of commercial agriculture and can provide fresh, healthy produce for your family.

Support sustainable businesses: When shopping, look for businesses that prioritize sustainability and ethical practices.

Choose energy-efficient appliances: When it's time to replace appliances, choose energy-efficient models that will save you money on energy bills and reduce your environmental impact.

Use eco-friendly transportation: Consider using electric or hybrid cars, or carpooling with others to reduce your carbon footprint.

Living sustainably on a budget is possible with some simple changes to your lifestyle. By reducing your energy consumption, using public transportation or walking/cycling, eating less meat, buying secondhand, and using reusable bags, water bottles, and containers, you can save money and reduce your environmental impact. Reducing waste and conserving resources through composting, buying in bulk, repairing instead of replacing, and using eco-friendly cleaning products can further reduce your environmental impact. Finally, finding eco-friendly solutions such as using solar power, planting a garden, supporting sustainable businesses, choosing energy-efficient appliances, and using eco-friendly transportation can also help you live a more sustainable lifestyle.

Living sustainably is not only good for the planet, but it's also good for your health and well-being. By reducing your exposure to harmful chemicals and pollutants, you can improve your overall health and reduce the risk of developing health problems such as respiratory issues, allergies, and cancer.

In addition to the practical benefits, living sustainably can also be a fulfilling and rewarding experience. When you take steps to reduce your environmental impact, you're making a positive contribution to the world and setting an example for others to follow. You can feel a sense of pride and satisfaction knowing that you're doing your part to create a better world for future generations.

Of course, living sustainably is not always easy. It can require some extra effort and sacrifice, and it may not always be the most convenient option. However, by making small changes over time, you can create habits that become second nature and make living sustainably a natural part of your daily life.

Building a sustainable lifestyle is an ongoing process that requires a commitment to change and a willingness to take action. By reducing your energy consumption, reducing waste and conserving resources, and finding eco-friendly solutions for everyday life, you can live sustainably on a budget without sacrificing quality of life. With a little effort and dedication, you can make a positive impact on the planet and create a better future for yourself and generations to come. So start today, and join the movement towards a more sustainable world.

Chapter 28: Overcoming Setbacks

Life is full of ups and downs, and the journey to financial stability is no exception. Budgeting can be a challenging process, and setbacks are bound to happen along the way. But setbacks don't have to derail your progress. In this chapter, we'll explore ways to deal with setbacks on your budgeting journey, strategies for overcoming setbacks, and how to stay motivated and committed through challenges.

Dealing with Setbacks on Your Budgeting Journey

Setbacks can take many forms when it comes to budgeting. It could be an unexpected expense that blows your budget, a job loss, or a dip in income. Whatever the cause, setbacks can be frustrating and discouraging. Here are some ways to deal with setbacks on your budgeting journey:

Don't beat yourself up: It's easy to get down on yourself when setbacks happen, but it's important to remember that setbacks are a normal part of the process. Don't beat yourself up or get discouraged.

Assess the situation: Take a step back and assess the situation. Determine the root cause of the setback and figure out what steps you need to take to address it.

Adjust your budget: If the setback is related to an unexpected expense, adjust your budget to accommodate it. Look for areas where you can cut back to make up for the expense.

Reevaluate your goals: Setbacks can be a good opportunity to reevaluate your financial goals. Determine if your goals are still realistic and adjust them if necessary.

Strategies for Overcoming Setbacks

Overcoming setbacks requires a combination of resilience and creativity. Here are some strategies for overcoming setbacks:

Find additional sources of income: If your setback is related to a dip in income, look for additional sources of income. This could be taking on a side hustle or freelance work.

Sell unused items: If you need to come up with some extra cash quickly, consider selling unused items around your home. This could be anything from clothes to electronics.

Negotiate bills: If you're struggling to make ends meet, try negotiating your bills. This could be negotiating your cable or internet bill, or even your rent.

Seek out support: Don't be afraid to seek out support from friends, family, or a financial advisor. Sometimes having someone to talk to and bounce ideas off of can make all the difference.

Stay Motivated and Committed through Challenges

Staying motivated and committed through challenges is key to overcoming setbacks and achieving your financial goals. Here are some ways to stay motivated and committed:

Celebrate small wins: Celebrating small wins along the way can help keep you motivated and focused. This could be anything from paying off a credit card to sticking to your budget for a month.

Visualize your goals: Visualizing your goals can help keep you motivated and committed. Create a vision board or write down your goals to help keep them top of mind.

Take care of yourself: Taking care of yourself is important when it comes to staying motivated and committed. Make sure to get enough sleep, eat healthy foods, and exercise regularly.

Stay connected to your why: Staying connected to your why - the reason why you're working towards financial stability - can help keep you motivated and committed. Write down your why and refer back to it when you're feeling discouraged.

Setbacks are an inevitable part of the budgeting journey, but they don't have to derail your progress. Dealing with setbacks requires resilience, creativity, and a willingness to adjust your approach as needed. Finding additional sources of income, selling unused items, negotiating bills, and seeking out support are all strategies for overcoming setbacks. Staying motivated and committed through challenges requires celebrating small wins, visualizing your goals, taking care of yourself, and staying connected to your why. Remember that setbacks are a normal part of the process, and with the right mindset and strategies, you can overcome them and continue on your journey towards financial stability.

It's important to remember that setbacks are not a reflection of your worth or abilities. It's easy to feel discouraged and beat yourself up when things don't go as planned, but this mindset will only hold you back. Instead, try to view setbacks as opportunities for growth and learning. Every setback is a chance to assess the situation, learn from it, and come up with a new plan of action.

Assessing the situation is key when it comes to dealing with setbacks. Take a step back and try to determine the root cause of the setback. Did you overspend in a certain category? Did you fail to plan for an unexpected expense? Did your income decrease? Once you've determined the root cause, you can come up with a plan to address it.

Chapter 29: Celebrating Your Successes

When it comes to achieving your goals, it's easy to focus on what's left to be done and forget to acknowledge your progress along the way. However, taking the time to celebrate your successes is important for staying motivated, maintaining a positive outlook, and reinforcing good habits. In this chapter, we'll explore the importance of celebrating your achievements, recognizing your progress and accomplishments, and rewarding yourself for your hard work.

The Importance of Celebrating Your Achievements

Celebrating your achievements is a vital part of the goal-setting process. Not only does it help to reinforce good habits and behaviors, but it also provides a much-needed sense of accomplishment and fulfillment. Here are a few reasons why celebrating your achievements is important:

Motivation: Celebrating your achievements can help to keep you motivated and focused on your goals. It provides a sense of progress and accomplishment that can keep you inspired to keep working towards your objectives.

Confidence: Celebrating your achievements can help to build your confidence and self-esteem. Recognizing your progress and accomplishments can help to reinforce positive beliefs about yourself and your abilities.

Reflection: Celebrating your achievements provides an opportunity for reflection. It allows you to take a step back and acknowledge how far you've come, which can provide valuable insight and perspective as you continue working towards your goals.

Recognizing Your Progress and Accomplishments

One of the most important aspects of celebrating your achievements is recognizing your progress and accomplishments. Here are a few tips for acknowledging your successes:

Keep track of your progress: Whether it's through a journal, spreadsheet, or some other means, keeping track of your progress is essential for recognizing your accomplishments. This can include anything from small wins to major milestones.

Share your successes with others: Sharing your successes with others can help to reinforce your accomplishments and build a sense of community. This can be as simple as telling a friend or family member about a recent achievement or sharing it on social media.

Reflect on your achievements: Take the time to reflect on your achievements and the progress you've made towards your goals. Consider what you've learned, the challenges you've overcome, and the skills you've developed.

Rewarding Yourself for Your Hard Work

Another important aspect of celebrating your successes is rewarding yourself for your hard work. This can help to reinforce good habits and behaviors and provide an added sense of motivation to continue working towards your goals. Here are a few ideas for rewarding yourself:

Treat yourself: Whether it's a special meal, a massage, or a new piece of clothing, treating yourself to something you enjoy can be a great way to reward yourself for your hard work.

Take a break: Sometimes the best reward is simply taking a break. Take a day off, go for a walk, or spend some time doing something you love.

Plan a trip or vacation: Planning a trip or vacation can be a great way to celebrate a major accomplishment. Whether it's a weekend getaway or a longer trip, it can provide a much-needed break and an opportunity to recharge.

Invest in yourself: Investing in yourself can be a great way to reward yourself for your hard work. This can include anything from taking a course or workshop to buying a new book or tool that can help you continue to grow and develop.

Celebrating your successes is an important part of the goal-setting process. It provides a sense of progress and accomplishment that can keep you motivated and focused on your goals. Recognizing your progress and accomplishments, sharing your successes with others, and rewarding yourself for your hard work are all important ways to celebrate your achievements. Remember to take the time to acknowledge your successes, no matter how small, and to reward yourself for your hard work. Celebrating your successes is a way to build confidence, motivation, and a positive outlook, which can help you continue to achieve your goals and dreams.

Chapter 30: Continuing Your Journey

Congratulations! You've made it to the end of this book on extreme budgeting. By now, you should have a solid understanding of what it takes to live a frugal lifestyle and how to take control of your finances. But the journey doesn't end here. In this final chapter, we'll discuss how to continue your journey towards extreme budgeting, create long-term habits and lifestyle changes, and maintain a positive mindset and commitment to your goals.

How to Continue Your Journey towards Extreme Budgeting

The first step to continuing your journey towards extreme budgeting is to maintain the same level of intensity and focus that you had when you started. It's easy to fall back into old habits and slip into a comfortable routine, but to truly achieve financial freedom, you must stay committed to your goals.

One way to maintain your momentum is to track your progress regularly. This will help you stay motivated and see how far you've come. Use spreadsheets, budgeting apps, or any other tool that works for you to keep track of your expenses, income, and savings. This will help you identify areas where you can cut back even further, and where you're already doing well.

Another way to continue your journey towards extreme budgeting is to keep learning. Read books, blogs, and articles on personal finance, and continue to educate yourself on the latest trends and strategies for saving money. Attend seminars, workshops, or webinars on the topic, and network with others who are on a similar journey. The more you learn, the more effective you'll be at managing your finances.

Creating Long-Term Habits and Lifestyle Changes

To make extreme budgeting a sustainable lifestyle, it's essential to create long-term habits and lifestyle changes. Here are some tips to help you do that:

Focus on your values: Identify your values and goals, and use them to guide your spending decisions. By aligning your spending with your values, you'll be more motivated to stick to your budget.

Practice mindfulness: Be mindful of your spending habits and try to identify the triggers that lead to impulsive purchases. Take a deep breath and think about your values and goals before making a purchase.

Make a plan: Create a long-term plan for achieving your financial goals, and break it down into smaller, achievable steps. Make a budget, set savings goals, and track your progress regularly.

Automate your finances: Automate as much of your finances as possible, such as bill payments and savings contributions. This will help you stay on track and avoid late fees or missed payments.

Practice self-discipline: Practice self-discipline by avoiding temptation and staying focused on your goals. This means saying "no" to unnecessary purchases, even if they seem tempting in the moment.

Maintaining a Positive Mindset and Commitment to Your Goals

Finally, maintaining a positive mindset and commitment to your goals is essential to continuing your journey towards extreme budgeting. Here are some tips to help you stay positive and focused:

Celebrate your successes: Take time to acknowledge your successes and celebrate your progress, no matter how small. This will help you stay motivated and focused on your goals.

Stay connected: Connect with others who are on a similar journey, whether it's through online forums, social media, or local meetups.

This will provide you with support and encouragement when you need it most.

Stay flexible: Be flexible and willing to adjust your budget or goals as necessary. Life is unpredictable, and you may need to make changes along the way.

Practice gratitude: Focus on what you have, rather than what you don't have. Practice gratitude by taking time each day to reflect on the things in your life that you're thankful for.

Remember that extreme budgeting is not just about cutting back on expenses; it's about living a more intentional and fulfilling life. By focusing on your values, practicing mindfulness, creating a long-term plan, automating your finances, and practicing self-discipline, you'll be able to make extreme budgeting a sustainable lifestyle.

Thank you for taking the time to read this book on extreme budgeting. I hope that you've found the information and advice useful and inspiring. Remember, the journey towards financial freedom is a marathon, not a sprint. It requires dedication, commitment, and a willingness to make changes to your lifestyle. But the rewards are worth it.

By taking control of your finances, you'll be able to reduce stress, achieve your goals, and live a more fulfilling life. You'll have more money to invest in your future, travel, or pursue your passions. You'll be able to give back to your community and support causes that are important to you.

But most importantly, by living a frugal lifestyle, you'll be able to appreciate the simple things in life and find joy in the little moments. You'll be able to live with intention and purpose, and make the most of every day.

So, I encourage you to take what you've learned in this book and apply it to your own life. Make a commitment to yourself to live a more intentional and fulfilling life, and don't give up when the going gets tough. Remember, every small step you take towards financial freedom is a step in the right direction.

Thank you again for reading this book, and I wish you all the best on your journey towards extreme budgeting and financial freedom.

Don't miss out!

Visit the website below and you can sign up to receive emails whenever SERGIO RIJO publishes a new book. There's no charge and no obligation.

https://books2read.com/r/B-A-COYW-FDRIC

BOOKS 2 READ

Connecting independent readers to independent writers.

Did you love *The Art of Extreme Budgeting: How to Live on Almost Nothing and Thrive*? Then you should read *30 Days to a Richer You: The Millionaire Success Habits That Will Change Your Life*[1] by SERGIO RIJO!

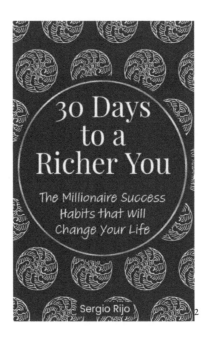

[2]

Are you tired of living paycheck to paycheck or struggling to make ends meet? Do you want to achieve financial success and live a life of abundance? If so, "30 Days to a Richer You" is the book for you.

In this comprehensive guide, you'll discover 30 actionable chapters filled with practical insights, exercises, and tips that will help you transform your life and achieve your goals. From developing a positive mindset and managing your time effectively to creating multiple streams of income and building a personal brand, each chapter is

1. https://books2read.com/u/4j5MNY

2. https://books2read.com/u/4j5MNY

designed to help you build the skills, habits, and mindset you need to achieve financial success.

Written in a friendly and easy-to-understand tone, "30 Days to a Richer You" is perfect for anyone who wants to take control of their finances and create a life of abundance. Whether you're a seasoned entrepreneur, a young professional just starting out, or simply someone who wants to improve their financial situation, this book is packed with valuable insights and practical exercises that will help you achieve your goals.

So why wait? Start your journey to a richer, more abundant life today with "30 Days to a Richer You."

Also by SERGIO RIJO

Rose Tattoo Designs: 300+ Designs to Inspire Your Next Tattoo
The Geometric Tattoo Handbook: A Complete Collection of 300+ Designs
Skull Tatoo Designs: Over 300 Tattoo Designs to Inspire You
Soulful: Unlocking the 16 Traits of Advanced Souls
Memory Mastery: The Proven System to Retain Information Effectively
Rise and Shine: A Guide to Kundalini Awakening for the Modern Spiritual Seeker
The Power of Presence: Connecting with Your Higher Self and Living with Purpose
Powerful Techniques for Mastering the Art of Influence: Proven Strategies to Exert Maximum Power and Persuasion
The Art of Remote Viewing: A Step-by-Step Guide to Unlocking Your Psychic Abilities
Money Magnetism: The Art of Attracting Abundance
The Happiness Handbook: A Practical Guide to Finding Joy and Fulfillment
The Smarter You: Proven Ways to Boost Your Intelligence
Appetite Control Strategies: The Secret to Successful Weight Loss
Off The Grid Living: A Comprehensive Guide to Sustainable and Self-Sufficient Living
The Ultimate Guide to Get Your Ex Back: A Step-by-Step Blueprint to Rekindle Love and Heal Your Relationship
Calm and Centered: Overcoming Anxiety and Panic Attacks Naturally
The Power Within: Boosting Self-Esteem and Confidence through Positive Self-Talk and Self-Care Practices
Grateful Living: Transform Your Life with the Power of Gratitude
Procrastination Uncovered: Understanding and Overcoming the Epidemic of Delay
Social Butterfly: Tips and Strategies for Conquering Shyness and Social Anxiety

Living with Purpose: Finding Meaning and Direction in Life

Breaking Free from Self-Sabotage: Overcoming Destructive Patterns and Achieving Your Goals

Uncovering the Shadows: A Journey through Shadow Work

The Science of Nutrition for Athletes: Understanding the Specific Nutritional Needs of Athletes for Optimal Performance and Recovery

The Magic of Saying No: How to Establish Boundaries and Take Charge of Your Life

Connecting with the Divine: Tools and Techniques for Powerful Prayer

Living in Harmony: The Complete Guide to Permaculture and Sustainable Living

Angelic Assistance: How to Connect with Your Guardian Angels and Spirit Guides for Support

Beyond Belief: Unraveling the Psychology of Ghosts and Hauntings

Transform Your Health with Intermittent Fasting: A Comprehensive Guide to Techniques and Benefits

Discover the Secrets of Lucid Dreaming: How to Use Your Dreams to Transform Your Life

Existential Crisis: Strategies for Finding Hope and Renewal in Life's Darkest Moments

The 12 Spiritual Laws of the Universe: A Comprehensive Guide to Achieving Personal Growth and Spiritual Enlightenment

The 144,000 Lightworkers: Healing and Awakening Humanity to Save the World

Defying Age: The Ultimate Guide to Living a Long and Healthy Life

Unlocking the Secrets of Astral Projection: Techniques for Successful Out-of-Body Experiences

Inner Child Healing: The Key to Overcoming Negative Beliefs, Self-Sabotage, and Unlocking Your True Potential

Raising Your Vibration: A Holistic Guide to Achieving Emotional and Spiritual Well-being

Psychic Vampires and Empaths: The Ultimate Guide to Protection and Healing with Energy, Crystals, Reiki, and More

Developing Clairvoyance: The Ultimate Guide to Unlocking Your Psychic Gifts and Connecting with the Spiritual World

Mastering Telekinesis: A Step-by-Step Guide to Developing Your Psychokinetic Abilities

Afterlife: Understanding Signs and Communication from Deceased Loved Ones

Navigating Spiritual Depression: Finding Meaning in the Dark Night of the Soul

Journey of the Old Soul: Navigating Life with Empathy, Wisdom, and Purpose

Third Eye Awakening: A Comprehensive Guide to Unlocking Your Inner Vision, Enhancing Intuition, and Activating the Pineal Gland for Spiritual Insight and Heightened Perception

Telepathy Unveiled: A Journey into the Secrets of Sending Telepathic Messages and Psychic Development

44 Letters from God: Divine Guidance for Life's Journey

Mastering Emotional Intelligence: Strategies for Cultivating Self-Awareness, Self-Regulation, and Empathy

The Power of Solitude: Embracing Alone Time for Self-Discovery and Fulfillment

The Ultimate Guide to Beekeeping: Tips and Tricks for Beginners

Akashic Records and Past Lives: Understanding How Past Lives Can Impact Your Present and Future

Mindful Eating for Emotional Freedom: Break the Cycle of Emotional Eating Habits

Stand-Up Comedy: A Guide to Writing and Performing with Confidence

The Art of Budget Travel: Techniques for Saving Money and Maximizing Experiences While Traveling

The Mystic Art of Alchemy: Understanding the Symbolism and Practice of Spiritual Transformation

The Power Within: A Guide to Self-Healing with Energy
Solo Travel: Techniques for Planning and Executing a Successful Solo Trip
The Art of Extreme Budgeting: How to Live on Almost Nothing and Thrive

About the Author

Join me on an adventure through captivating stories! I'm Sergio Rijo, a passionate writer with 20 years of experience in crafting books across genres. Let's explore new worlds together and get hooked from start to finish.